Pride of Puerto Rico

Pride of Puerto Rico

The Life of Roberto Clemente

PAUL ROBERT WALKER

An Odyssey Book

Harcourt, Inc.

Orlando Austin New York San Diego London

For information about permission to reproduce
selections from this book, please write Permissions,
Houghton Mifflin Harcourt Publishing Company
215 Park Avenue South, NY, NY 10003.

www.hmhbooks.com

Library of Congress Cataloging-in-Publication Data
Walker, Paul Robert.
Pride of Puerto Rico: the life of Roberto Clemente/Paul Robert Walker.
p.   cm.
"An Odyssey Book."
Summary: A biography of the baseball superstar from Puerto Rico
who, before his untimely death in a 1972 airplane crash, was noted
for his achievements on and off the baseball field.
ISBN 978-0-15-263420-9
1. Clemente, Roberto, 1934–1972—Juvenile literature.   2. Baseball
players—Puerto Rico—Biography—Juvenile literature.   3. Pittsburgh
Pirates (Baseball team)—Juvenile literature.   [1. Clemente,
Roberto, 1934–1972.   2. Baseball players.   3. Blacks—Biography.
4. Puerto Rico—Biography.]   I. Title.
GV865.C45W35   1991
796.357'092—dc20   [B][92]   90-45521

Printed in the United States of America

DOC 20 19 18 17
4500365132

CONTENTS

v

Pride of Puerto Rico

1

The Way of the Jíbaro

Roberto closed his eyes and imagined himself in the great stadium of San Juan. There were men on first and third with two outs in the bottom of the ninth. His team was losing, 5–3. A double would tie the game. A home run would win it. Everything depended on him.

He stepped confidently into the batter's box and took two level practice swings. Then he cocked his bat and waited for the pitch. The white ball came toward him in slow motion, its seams spinning clearly in the air. His bat was a blur as he whipped it around and smashed the ball over the left-field fence!

"Clemente!" cried a voice behind him. "Are you playing or dreaming?"

Roberto opened his eyes and stared seriously at the boy who had spoken. "I am playing," he said.

It was a warm tropical evening in Puerto Rico.

Roberto Clemente was playing with a group of boys on a muddy field in Barrio San Antón. It was nothing at all like the great stadium in San Juan. There were bumps and puddles, and the outfield was full of trees. The bat in Roberto's hand was a thick stick cut from the branch of a guava tree. The bases were old coffee sacks. The ball was a tightly knotted bunch of rags.

The boys on the field were black and white and many shades of brown. They shouted at each other in Spanish, encouraging their teammates, taunting their opponents. This was an important game between the boys of Barrio San Antón and a team from Barrio Martín Gonzalez.

Eight-year-old Roberto Clemente was one of the youngest and smallest boys on the field. As he stepped up to the plate, the thick guava stick felt very heavy in his hands. It was a great honor to represent his neighborhood. Everything depended on him.

Roberto looked over at third base, where his brother Andrés stood waiting to score. He looked at first, where another boy waited impatiently, hoping to score the tying run. Then he took a deep breath, cocked his bat, and waited for the pitch.

The big ball of rags arched toward him as if it were in slow motion. Roberto swung with all his strength, but instead of sailing over the left-field fence, the ball rolled weakly back to the mound. The pitcher fielded it easily and threw to first for the final out. The game was over. San Antón had lost by a score of 5–3. Roberto stood alone while the other players left the field. He could feel tears trickling down his cheeks, and he was ashamed to cry in front of the older boys. His brother Andrés called to him from a few feet away. "Momen!" he said. "Are you going to stand there all night? It's time for supper."

"You go ahead," said Roberto. "I promised to meet Papá."

Roberto was the youngest of seven children in the Clemente family. There were six boys and one girl. When he was very little, Roberto's sister Rosa called him "Momen." It didn't mean anything in particular. It was just a made-up word, but to his family Roberto was always Momen.

Roberto's father, Don Melchor Clemente, worked as a foreman in the sugar fields. Sugar was the most important crop for the people of Puerto Rico. At harvest time, the sharp green stalks of sugar cane stood twice as tall as a man.

From sunrise to sunset, the men of Barrio San Antón worked in the fields, cutting the thick stalks of cane with their sharp machetes. It was hard, back-breaking work and the pay was $2.00 per week.

Don Clemente was more fortunate than most. As a foreman, he earned $4.00 a week. He and his wife, Doña Luisa, also ran a small store, selling meat and other goods to the workers on the sugar plantation. There was no money for luxuries like real baseballs and bats, but there was always plenty of rice and beans on the Clemente family table.

As he walked down the dirt road between the tall fields of sugar cane, Roberto thought about the game. He had failed his team. Perhaps he was not good enough to play with the bigger boys. Perhaps he would never be good enough. Once again he could feel the tears in his eyes.

It was late in the evening now, and the sun was setting over the fields like a great orange ball of fire. Roberto reached a high point in the road and looked for his father. Suddenly his tears disappeared. There, above the tall stalks of cane, sat Don Melchor Clemente, riding slowly on his paso fino horse.

"Papá! Papá! Wait for me!"

Roberto ran through the cane field to where his father was riding. Don Melchor reached down and helped Roberto climb into the saddle behind him. Don Melchor Clemente was very proud to own such a fine horse. And Roberto was proud to ride behind his father.

"So, Momen," Don Melchor said as they rode home through the fields, "you come at last. I thought you had forgotten."

"Forgive me, Papá," said Roberto. "I was playing baseball."

"Ah, and how was the baseball?"

Roberto was silent for a moment. He thought again of the weak ground ball that ended the game for Barrio San Antón. He did not want to tell his father of his failure, but he knew that Don Melchor Clemente was a man who accepted only the truth. Finally he took a deep breath and spoke. "I lost the game, Papá."

"Hmmm," Don Melchor said. "That is very interesting." Father and son continued to ride in silence. Then Don Melchor spoke again. "I do not know very much about this baseball," he said. "But I know that there are many players on a team. I do not understand how one small boy can lose the game."

"But Papá," said Roberto, "I was our only hope. I could have been the hero. Instead I was the last man out. The other boys will never ask me to play again."

They were out of the sugar fields now and riding

slowly down the red dirt road that ran through Barrio San Antón. Don Melchor looked straight ahead as he guided his horse toward home. His words were strong and clear in the evening air.

"Momen," he said, "I want you to listen very carefully. Perhaps the other boys will ask you. Perhaps they will not. It does not matter. There are other boys and other teams, but there is only one life. I want you to be a good man. I want you to work hard. And I want you to be a serious person."

Don Melchor stopped his horse in the road. They were only a few hundred yards from home now, and Roberto could clearly see the wood and concrete house set in a grove of banana trees. Barrio San Antón lay on the outskirts of the city of Carolina. To the west was the capital city of San Juan. To the east were the cloud-covered slopes of El Yunque, barely visible in the fading light.

"Remember who you are," Don Melchor said. "Remember where you come from. You are a Jíbaro. Like me. Like my father and my father's father. We are a proud people. Hundreds of years ago, we went into the mountains because we refused to serve the Spanish noblemen. In the wilderness, we learned to live off the land. Now, even in the sugar fields, we do not forget what we have learned.

"A man must be honest. He must work for what

6

he needs. He must share with his brothers who have less. This is the way of the Jíbaro. This is the way of dignity." Don Melchor paused for a moment. It was dark now, and supper was waiting. "Do you understand, my son?" he asked.

Roberto thought carefully about his father's words. Then he spoke, quietly but firmly. "Yes, Papá," he said, "I understand."

2

One Penny a Day

Puerto Rico is very small and very beautiful. It is a land of sunshine and sandy beaches, tropical trees and brightly colored birds. It is one of the West Indies, a group of islands that stretch like a sparkling necklace from the southern tip of Florida to the coast of South America. To the north is the Atlantic Ocean. To the south is the Caribbean Sea.

The name "Puerto Rico" means "Rich Port." Today, many Puerto Ricans live comfortable lives. But when Roberto Clemente was born in 1934, the riches of the island were in the hands of a few American companies who owned the sugar fields. For most of the people, life was a constant struggle.

During World War II, life became even harder for the people of Puerto Rico. German submarines hid in the deep blue waters of the Caribbean Sea, sinking ships that carried food and supplies for the tiny island. But even in the hardest times, Don

Melchor and Doña Luisa made certain their children had enough to eat. When the children were finished, the parents would eat what was left.

"Papá," Roberto asked one evening, "may I have a bicycle?"

Don Melchor considered the request of his youngest son. Even in the middle of a war, he thought, children must think of their toys. "Earn it," he said.

"But Papá," Roberto replied, "how can I earn so much money?"

"You will find a way."

Doña Luisa overheard their conversation as she cleared away the supper dishes. "Momen," she said, "Señora Martín is looking for a boy to carry her milk can back and forth to the store. She is willing to pay one penny a day."

That evening, Roberto went to the neighbor's house and agreed to take the job. The next morning, he woke at dawn, dressed quickly, and went to pick up the empty milk can Señora Martín had left on her porch. It was a half mile to the small store where the people of Barrio San Antón bought their milk. As Roberto carried the empty milk can along the road, he felt good inside. The birds were singing in the trees and the sun was rising over the sugar fields. It was a beautiful morning.

On the way back, the morning did not seem so

beautiful. The sun was already hot, and the full can was a heavy load for a nine-year-old boy. Roberto's muscles ached and he could feel the salty sweat running down his face. But when Señora Martín smiled and placed the penny in his hand, he forgot his aches and ran happily to Doña Luisa's kitchen.

"Mamá!" he cried. "Look!"

Doña Luisa smiled brightly as Roberto held out the penny he had earned. "*Bueno*, Momen," she said. "Now you are a working man." Roberto's mother reached up and took a large glass jar down from a kitchen shelf. "Here," she said as she removed the lid, "drop the penny in the jar and I will keep your money in the kitchen."

Roberto did as he was told and watched his mother place the jar back on the high shelf. "It looks so small," he said, "all alone in that big jar."

Doña Luisa smiled and patted Roberto's cheek. "Don't worry, Momen," she said, "it will grow."

For the next three years, Roberto rose every morning at dawn and carried the milk can for Señora Martín. It was hard waking up so early, and sometimes he felt tired during his long day at school. But he always had enough energy to play baseball when the school day was over.

As the pennies in the big glass jar began to grow, so did Roberto. He was no longer one of the smallest boys on the team. He was still very skinny, but he was tall and his muscles were strong. He could smash the big ball of rags all over the neighborhood field.

Sometimes, when he was not in school or playing baseball, Roberto would earn a few extra coins working for his father. Don Melchor owned an old truck that he used to carry sand and gravel for construction work. Roberto and his brothers worked long hours loading and unloading the truck.

Finally, after three years of hard work, there was $27.00 in the big glass jar. Roberto took the money he had earned and bought a secondhand bicycle. He cleaned it and polished it until the metal sparkled in the sun. Don Melchor and Doña Luisa watched proudly as Roberto pedaled down the dirt road in Barrio San Antón.

"That Momen," said Doña Luisa, "when he sets his mind to something, he does it."

During the years he saved for his bicycle, Roberto would sometimes take a few pennies from the glass jar to buy a hard rubber ball. All day long, he would squeeze the ball to strengthen his wrists and arms. At night, he would lay in bed, listening to baseball games on the radio and bouncing the rubber ball against the wall.

"Momen!" his mother cried. "You are driving me crazy with that ball!"

"I am sorry, Mamá," said Roberto. "I am listening to baseball."

"Baseball!" Doña Luisa muttered to herself. "That boy is going to turn into a baseball."

In his room, Roberto crouched closer to the radio and listened to the game from Sixto Escobar Stadium in San Juan. During the winter, many players from the United States came to play in Puerto Rico. There were great stars from the Negro Leagues like Josh Gibson and Satchel Paige. There were light-skinned major leaguers and Puerto Rican players of many colors. In the United States, blacks and whites could not play on the same team, but in Puerto Rico a player was judged by his talent, not by his color.

Roberto's favorite player was Monte Irvin, a star outfielder in the American Negro Leagues. During the winter, he played for the San Juan Senators. Irvin was not only a great hitter, but he could throw like no one else in the game. As Roberto listened to the radio announcer telling of Monte Irvin's miraculous plays, he squeezed the hard rubber ball and imagined his powerful arm throwing a baserunner out at the plate.

"Momen, come here."

Roberto tore himself away from the radio and went to his father.

"Yes, Papá?"

"I want you to go into San Juan and buy a lottery ticket. Here is the money for the ticket, and here is money for the bus."

"Yes, Papá."

Roberto took the money and placed it carefully in his pocket. He was proud that his father would trust him with such an important task. The lottery was very exciting. Who knows? Perhaps he would buy a winning ticket. Perhaps they would all be rich.

"Be careful with the money, and come straight home after buying the ticket."

"Yes, Papá."

Roberto rode the bus along the dirt highway that led to San Juan. The capital city was only fourteen miles away, but to Roberto it seemed like another world. He had visited San Juan before, but always with his parents or older brothers. This was his first time alone.

As he approached the city, the houses were closer and closer together. Soon, the streets were crowded with people. About a mile before the place where the lottery tickets were sold, the bus stopped at Sixto

Escobar Stadium where the San Juan Senators were playing the team from Caguas. Even inside the bus, Roberto could see the bright lights of the stadium and hear the noise of the crowd.

Roberto quickly considered the situation. He had promised his father to come straight home after buying the lottery ticket. But he had said nothing about stopping *before* he bought the ticket. Roberto jumped off the bus and stood outside the stadium, watching the game through the fence. His heart beat quickly with excitement. An hour ago, he was listening to the game on the radio. Now it was here before his eyes.

The Senators were batting, and Roberto decided to wait until Monte Irvin came to the plate. Finally, his hero emerged from the dugout, swinging three bats in his powerful arms. He tossed two of them aside and stepped into the batter's box. Roberto stared in wonder. Those arms are as big as my legs, he thought.

The pitcher leaned back and fired a fastball on the outside corner of the plate. Irvin swung with all his might and lifted a high pop-up behind home plate. It was the highest foul ball Roberto had ever seen. He watched as the wind blew it back over the grandstand and out of the park. It was coming right to him! Roberto backed away from the fence and put his hands together. Smack! The hard leather ball landed safely in his hands.

Roberto went back to the fence and watched as Monte Irvin singled up the middle. Then he walked the last mile to buy his father's lottery ticket. As he rode the bus back to Barrio San Antón, he held the baseball tightly in his hand. That night he placed it underneath his pillow. Perhaps his father would win the lottery, he thought. Perhaps he would not. Either way, Roberto knew he was lucky.

3

Where Are You Going, Momen?

"Where are you going, Momen?"

Roberto smiled at his mother as he rushed out the door. "To play baseball, Mamá!"

"Don't be late for supper!" Doña Luisa stood in the doorway and watched Roberto disappear across the road. It was only 11:00 in the morning, but she knew she would not see him for the rest of the day. Why do I even ask? she thought. Of course he is going to play baseball.

It was the summer of 1948, and Roberto was fourteen years old. The war had been over for three years, and life was a little easier for the people of Puerto Rico. There was good chicken and roast pork to go along with the rice and beans on the family table. Occasionally, there was even money for other things. As Roberto walked to the neighborhood field, he carried a real baseball bat over his shoulder.

One of Roberto's friends had a real softball. It was exciting for the boys of Barrio San Antón to play with good equipment. All day long they pounded the white softball around the field until it was caked and covered with mud. They did not even count the innings. They played and played through the morning, through the afternoon, and into the evening.

With his new bat, Roberto smashed ten home runs during the long game. At shortstop, he made wonderful catches and powerful throws to first base. It was only six years since he first played with the neighborhood team, but now he was one of the best players on the field.

Finally, the evening grew so dark that the boys could no longer see the ball. Roberto tossed his bat over his shoulder and headed for home. He felt tired but good. He had played baseball for eight straight hours.

"You are late, Momen." Doña Luisa looked up angrily as Roberto entered the kitchen door. It was now completely dark and the rest of the family had already finished dinner.

"Forgive me, Mamá," he said. "I was playing baseball, and I forgot the time."

"Baseball! I am sick and tired of this baseball! All day! Every day! You do not even bother to eat!"

Roberto looked down at the empty dishes on the table. "It's all right," he said. "I'm not hungry."

"Not hungry!" cried Doña Luisa. "Tell me, Momen. What kind of boy can live without food?"

Roberto continued to stare at the table. "I am sorry, Mamá."

"I will show you what is sorry!" With a powerful flash of her strong right arm, Roberto's mother grabbed the bat out of his hand and stormed into the living room where Don Melchor was sitting quietly. Without a glance at her husband or her son, she knelt in front of the fireplace and began to make a fire. Roberto stared in amazement as she lit the crumpled paper and added pieces of wood until he could feel the heat in the room. Finally, Doña Luisa tossed Roberto's bat into the flames.

"No, Mamá!" Roberto cried. "Please!" Scrambling around his mother, Roberto reached into the fire and rescued his burning bat. The wood was black and hot in his hands. He looked at Don Melchor, who sat unsmiling in his chair.

"Papá?" said Roberto.

"Momen," Don Melchor replied, "your mother made a very fine dinner."

Roberto looked down at the bat in his hands. "Yes, Papá," he said.

In the kitchen, Roberto hungrily ate the cold chicken and rice that Doña Luisa laid on the table. "Forgive me, Mamá," he said. "I will not be late again."

Doña Luisa smiled. Her anger was forgotten now. "Momen," she said, "there is so much more than baseball. You must study hard. Someday you will go to the university. Perhaps you will be a great engineer. Our people need roads and bridges and buildings. Perhaps you will build them."

Roberto sat quietly, thinking about his mother's words. "Mamá," he said at last, "I believe that God wants me to play baseball."

Doña Luisa stared at her youngest son. "Momen," she said, "who are we to know the will of God?"

"But if it is so?" Roberto asked. "If it is so, will you give me your blessing?"

For a moment, Doña Luisa was silent. She closed her eyes and listened to the sounds of the night outside the Clemente house. Finally, she looked kindly at Roberto. "Sí, Momen," she said, "if it is so, I will give you my blessing."

Señora Cáceres stood behind her wooden desk and watched her new students file into the room. "You may choose your own seats," she said. "But remember, that will be your seat for the whole semester."

It was the first day of school at Vizcarrondo High School in the city of Carolina. Señora Cáceres waited until the students were settled into their seats before beginning the lesson.

"Today we will try to speak in English," she said. "I know that will be difficult for many of you, but the only way to improve is to practice. Now, who can tell me something about the history of Puerto Rico?"

Several students eagerly raised their hands. Señora Cáceres pointed to a pretty girl in the front row. The girl stood up and spoke in careful English.

"Puerto Rico was discovered by Christopher Columbus in 1493. He claim the island for Spain. The first governor was Ponce de León."

"Very good," said Señora Cáceres as the girl sat down. "And when did Puerto Rico become part of the United States?"

Again the same students raised their hands. Señora Cáceres looked around the room. Roberto sat in the very last row, his eyes staring at the floor. He had studied English in grammar school, but, like most of his friends, he could not really use it in conversation.

"Come now," said Señora Cáceres. "You'll never learn unless you try it."

Very slowly, Roberto raised his hand. Señora Cáceres smiled and pointed to the back row. As Roberto stood up and began to answer, he kept his eyes cast down toward the floor. His voice was very quiet. "We . . . become . . . United States . . . 1898," he said. "We are American . . . cities."

A few of the students laughed at Roberto's poor pronunciation. Señora Cáceres smiled and gently corrected him. "Citizens," she said. "We are American citizens."

As Roberto took his seat, Señora Cáceres noticed a group of girls giggling and whispering in the corner. "Yes," she thought, "this quiet one is a very handsome boy."

Señora Cáceres soon discovered that her quiet student was not so shy on the playing field. Roberto was the greatest athlete in the history of Vizcarrondo High School. He was not only a star on the baseball diamond; he also excelled in track and field. He could throw the javelin 190 feet, triple-jump 45 feet, and high-jump over 6 feet. Many people hoped that Roberto would represent Puerto Rico in the Olympic Games. But despite his success in track and field, baseball was his greatest love.

Bam! Bam! Bam!

Roberto stood on the muddy field in Barrio San Antón with a broomstick in his hands. Next to the boy on the pitcher's mound was a pile of old tin cans. Roberto and his friends were using the tin cans for batting practice. According to the rules, Roberto could bat until the pitcher struck him out. The rest of the boys had to wait in the field for their turn at bat.

Frowning in frustration, the pitcher reached down and picked up another tin can. Once again, he leaned back and tried to fire the can past Roberto at the plate. Bam! Once again, Roberto smashed the can into the outfield.

"Hey, Clemente!" yelled a boy at shortstop. "Why don't you give someone else a chance to bat?"

Roberto smiled seriously and shrugged his shoulders. "First you must strike me out," he said.

On the dirt road that ran along the field, Señor Roberto Marín leaned against his car and watched carefully. It was almost sunset, but he could still see the boys clearly in the twilight. Señor Marín was a man who loved baseball, and he was always looking for new talent. As part of his job with the Sello Rojo Rice Company, he was putting together an all-star softball team to represent the company in a big tournament in San Juan.

"*Caramba!*" said Señor Marín. "That boy can really hit those cans." Señor Marín walked across the field to Roberto. "Who are you?" he asked.

"I am Momen," Roberto replied.

"Well, I tell you, Momen. Why don't you come over to Carolina and try out for my softball team? I think we can use you."

The next day, Roberto rode his bicycle into Carolina to try out for the softball team. It was only a couple of miles from Barrio San Antón to the field in Carolina, but it was a big step for Roberto. He was only a freshman in high school. Most of the other players were much older.

"Don't worry," said Señor Marín, "if you can hit a softball like you hit those tin cans, you'll do all right."

Roberto waited patiently at the plate as the softball sailed toward him in the evening air. At the last moment, he whipped his bat around and smashed the ball into right field. Señor Marín smiled with satisfaction. I know a ballplayer when I see one, he thought.

For the next two years, Roberto played for the Sello Rojo softball team. At first he played shortstop, but Señor Marín decided he would be better in the outfield. Soon Roberto was entertaining the softball fans of Carolina and San Juan with his brilliant catches and powerful arm.

Although softball was his favorite game, Roberto also played hardball in the San Juan youth league. When he was sixteen, he played for the Ferdinand Juncos team in the Puerto Rican amateur league. Here the competition was stronger, and the quality of the players was similar to the Class-A minors in the professional leagues of the United States.

One day, Don Melchor came to watch his son. Roberto's father knew very little about baseball. Unfortunately, Roberto's teammates did not hit very well that day. Time after time, they struck out or grounded weakly to the infielders. But when Roberto came to bat, he smashed a long home run and ran at full speed around the bases.

After the game, Roberto approached his father proudly. "Tell me, Papá," he said, "how did you like the baseball?"

"Very interesting," Don Melchor replied. "But no wonder you are always tired! The other players just run to first base and walk back to the dugout. You run all the way around the bases!"

Don Melchor smiled slightly at his own joke. Then his face turned serious. "Momen," he said, "perhaps someday you will run to the major leagues."

4

Tell the Man I Will Sign

Al Campanis stood on the playing field at Sixto Escobar Stadium and looked at the semicircle of eager young men waiting for his instructions. Many of them were still teenagers, standing nervously in the baggy uniforms of local amateur teams. There were 72 in all. And every one of them wanted to be a big-league ballplayer.

"All right," Campanis said, "you all know why you're here. Señor Zorilla and the Santurce baseball club have been kind enough to invite me down here to take a look. There's no reason to be nervous. Just do your best and show me what you've got."

Campanis was a scout for the Brooklyn Dodgers. For the past three years, he'd been traveling to Puerto Rico, Cuba, and the Dominican Republic looking for talented players. It was 1952, and American baseball was changing. Five years earlier, Jackie Robinson had become the first black man to play on a major-league team. In 1951, a black player from Cuba named Minnie Minoso starred for the Chicago White Sox. Suddenly, the dark-skinned boys of the Puerto Rican barrios had a reason to dream.

"Everybody in the outfield," Campanis ordered. "I want to see you throw to the plate."

As the boys jogged out into center field, Campanis took his position in foul territory. Beside him was a coach with a clipboard. Each of the boys wore a number pinned to the back of his shirt. On the coach's clipboard was a list of their names and numbers.

Campanis watched as boy after boy launched long lobs from deep center field. These local tryouts were usually a waste of time. Still, he thought, you never know. Suddenly one of the boys caught his attention. A skinny kid leaned back in deep center field and fired a perfect strike to the plate. Al Campanis could hardly believe his eyes.

"*Uno más!*" he shouted.

Once again, the boy cocked his right arm and fired. The ball flew on a perfect line and smacked the hard leather of the catcher's glove.

"Who is that kid?" Campanis asked.

The coach standing beside him looked at the number on the boy's back and compared it with the list on his clipboard. "Clemente," he said. "Roberto Clemente."

When all the boys had taken their throws, Mr. Campanis took out his stopwatch and timed them in the 60-yard dash. The world's record was 6.1 seconds. In his full baseball uniform, Roberto ran the distance in 6.4 seconds. Once again, Al Campanis could not believe his eyes.

"*Uno más,*" he said. Roberto walked back to the starting line and ran again. Campanis stared at the stopwatch in amazement—6.4 seconds twice in a row.

"Thank you, gentlemen," Campanis said to the rest of the boys. "You may go. Clemente, I want to see you hit."

Roberto stepped into the batting cage. Campanis watched as the skinny kid in the baggy uniform smashed line drives all over the field. After a few minutes, the scout noticed that Roberto was standing too far from the plate. He ordered the pitcher to keep the ball outside.

The way he's standing, Campanis thought, he'll never be able to reach it.

The pitcher leaned back and fired a high outside fastball. Roberto swung with both feet off the ground and smashed the ball up the middle.

"What do you think?"

Al Campanis turned to look at the man who had spoken. It was Señor Marín, the man who had first discovered Roberto's talent. Both Campanis and Marín knew that Roberto was major-league material. But Campanis did his best to hide his excitement. Roberto was still in high school, and the Dodgers could not yet legally sign him to a contract.

"He has great tools," Campanis said, "but he needs polish."

"*Caramba!* What a pair of hands!" Pedrín Zorilla eyed the skinny, quiet boy standing in the living room of Zorilla's beachfront home in the town of Manatí. It was a few months after the tryout in Sixto Escobar Stadium. Roberto Clemente had just turned eighteen.

"I tell you, Pedrín, he's a gem. An unpolished gem," said Señor Marín.

Zorilla continued to stare at Roberto's hands. Zorilla was the owner of the Santurce Crabbers, one of the top teams in the Puerto Rican winter league. He had seen many great ballplayers in his time, but he had never seen a young boy with such long, powerful fingers.

"Shots, Pedrín. You remember the tryout. He hit nothing but line shots."

Zorilla looked at his friend, Señor Marín. Then he looked again at Roberto Clemente. "A tryout is one thing," he said. "A game is another. I would like to see him play."

A few days later, Pedrín Zorilla watched Roberto in action with the Ferdinand Juncos team in the Puerto Rican amateur league. In the second inning, Roberto knocked in two runs with a long double. Two innings later, he followed with a 400-foot triple. In the seventh, he smashed another double. In the top of the ninth, his perfect throw from center field nailed a runner at the plate.

"Well, Marín," said Señor Zorilla, "we can give him a $400 bonus and maybe $40.00 a week until he learns to wear a uniform."

Roberto sat silently on Señor Zorilla's flagstone patio. It was a warm sunny day, and a fresh breeze was blowing off the Atlantic. Although he listened respectfully as the two older men discussed his contract, inside Roberto was bubbling over with excitement. A professional baseball player! He could hardly believe his ears.

"What should I do?" Roberto asked as Señor Marín drove him to Barrio San Antón. "What should I do?"

The older man watched the road ahead as he

considered Roberto's question. It had been three years since he first saw Roberto hitting tin cans in Barrio San Antón. He had done his best to help the young boy develop his natural talent. He drove him to and from the games. He praised him when he played well, and he encouraged him when he did not. He cared for Roberto as if he were his own son. But this was a decision he did not have the right to make.

"We'll discuss it with your father," he said finally. "We'll talk it over, and he'll decide."

That evening, Don Melchor looked over the piece of paper in his hand. "Very interesting," he said. "I must think about this." Don Melchor showed Roberto's contract to one of his neighbors. "They are offering Roberto $400 to play baseball," he said.

During his many years of hard work in the sugar fields, Don Melchor had never found time to learn how to read. He listened carefully as the neighbor read the whole contract out loud. "What do you think?" he asked.

"When they offer $400," the neighbor replied, "it means he is worth much more. Don't sign a thing."

The next day, Don Melchor and Señor Marín went to the house of Pedrín Zorilla. Don Melchor looked around the beautiful living room. There are many fine things in this house, he thought. This Señor Zorilla is a wealthy man.

"I think you can give more money for my boy," said Don Melchor. "He is a fine player."

Pedrín Zorilla looked at the wiry black man who stood before him. Don Melchor Clemente was 71 years old, but he had the strength of a much younger man. Zorilla admired Don Melchor's faith in the talents of his son. But he also knew that $400 was a good bonus for a Puerto Rican player. Many boys signed for $100 or less.

"Frankly," said Señor Zorilla, "if you want more money, I have no interest in him. I think he's good, but he's got no record to prove it."

That night, the Clemente family sat around the dinner table. They were all very excited about Roberto's chance to play professional baseball. "Don't worry," Don Melchor said. "They will offer more. We will just have to wait."

Roberto stared down at the roast pork on his plate. He did not feel very hungry. All his life he had dreamed about playing professional baseball. Now he was offered a chance. What difference did a few dollars make? Slowly, he looked up from the plate and directly into his father's eyes.

"Papá," he said, "I don't want to wait. I want to play."

Don Melchor stared at Roberto. In eighteen years, his youngest son had never spoken to him like this. It was always "Yes, Papá" or "Your blessing, Papá." For a moment, Don Melchor was angry. "What do you mean you do not want to wait? If I say you wait, then you wait."

"But, Papá," Roberto replied, "you always say a man must work for what he needs. Their offer is fair. When I prove myself, then they will pay me more."

Don Melchor silently considered Roberto's words. No, he thought, there is no reason for anger. Momen has learned his lessons well. It is good for a boy to become a man.

"All right," he said seriously, "tell the man I will sign."

5

Wearing the Uniform

Roberto sat on the hard wooden bench and held his head in his hands. The Santurce Crabbers were playing the team from Ponce, a city in the south of Puerto Rico. The Crabbers were leading 7–5 in the bottom of the eighth inning, but Roberto was not very happy. It was already two months into the season, and so far he had only played in a few games as a pinch hitter or a late-inning defensive replacement.

If this is professional baseball, Roberto thought, I would be better off buying a ticket and watching it from the grandstand. At least there I'd have a comfortable seat.

Santurce had many fine players from the major leagues. The Puerto Rican fans take their baseball very seriously, and Santurce was fighting for the league championship. There was not much opportunity for an eighteen-year-old rookie who was still in high school. But this didn't make Roberto feel any better. He was good at playing baseball. He was not very good at sitting on the bench.

That night, Roberto spoke to Señor Marín as he drove him home from the game. "If I don't play tomorrow," he said, "I quit."

"Chico!" said Señor Marín, "what are you talking about?"

"I mean it," said Roberto. "I am here to play, not to sit."

"Hmmm," said Señor Marín. "I will speak to Señor Zorilla."

"The young one wants to play."

"You know how I feel about rookies," said Pedrín Zorilla. "We have many great pitchers in this league. I tell you, Marín, a boy like Clemente strikes out three or four times in a row and suddenly he starts asking questions. 'Can I hit? Can I really play?' It is important he does not give himself the wrong answers."

"But the boy is desperate," said Señor Marín. "You cannot keep him on the bench."

"Listen, Marín," said Señor Zorilla. "I am the man who pays his salary. Clemente plays when I say he plays."

That night, Señor Marín drove Roberto to the

ballpark. "Take it easy, Chico," said the older man. "Your day will come. Señor Zorilla says he will play you soon."

"You're dragging your left foot. You're bailing out. That's OK for the inside pitches, but you'll never be able to hit the outside curveball."

Roberto listened carefully to his manager, Buster Clarkson. Clarkson was a husky shortstop who had been a great star in the Negro Leagues. He had just finished his only major-league season with the Boston Braves. Now he was playing and managing with the Santurce Crabbers.

"Here, let's try this." Clarkson laid a bat on the ground behind Roberto's feet. "Now I want you to swing without touching the bat with your left foot." Clarkson nodded to the pitcher. "Nothing but outside curves," he shouted.

For twenty minutes, Roberto stood in the batter's box and practiced hitting the outside curveballs without dragging his left foot. At first, it was very difficult. Ever since he was a small boy in Barrio San Antón, he had dragged his left foot away from the pitch. But this was not a guava stick in his hands, and the pitchers in the Puerto Rican winter league did not throw a big ball of rags.

"That's it," said Clarkson, "step right into the

pitch." The veteran player watched as Roberto struggled to adjust his batting style. Soon the skinny eighteen-year-old was smashing the outside curveball for line drives to right and center field.

"Now you've got it," Clarkson said. "Keep it up and you'll be as good as Willie Mays."

When Roberto was finished with batting practice, Clarkson watched the young player run smoothly toward the outfield. He turned to the coach beside him and smiled. "That kid's gonna be all right," he said. "He listens, he works hard, and he doesn't make the same mistake twice."

Late in the season, the Santurce Crabbers were playing in Caguas. It was the top of the ninth inning, and the Crabbers had the bases loaded with two outs. Santurce was down by two runs. This was their last chance.

The next man up was Bob Thurman. Thurman was a solid batter who later played in the major leagues, but he had trouble hitting left-handed pitchers and Caguas had a lefty on the mound. Buster Clarkson called Thurman back from the on-deck circle and looked down the bench at Clemente. "Grab yourself a bat," he said.

As Roberto stepped up to the plate, he looked

around the stadium. There were thousands of fans in the stands. Although it was night, the field was as bright as the middle of the day. Roberto thought for a moment of the muddy field in Barrio San Antón. Then he stepped into the batter's box.

He took two level practice swings, cocked his bat, and waited for the pitch. The white ball came toward him in a blur. It was not in slow motion as he had imagined when he was a boy. It was fast. Very fast. Roberto swung wildly and missed.

Roberto took a deep breath and set himself for the next pitch. This time he was ready. With a powerful flick of his wrists, he reached out and smashed the ball down the right-field line. He rounded first base at full speed and slid into second with a double. All three runs scored. Santurce had taken the lead.

From then on, Roberto was given more and more chances to play. The next year, in his second season with the Crabbers, he broke into the starting lineup. Roberto thrilled the Puerto Rican fans with his dazzling catches and powerful arm in right field, and he batted a solid .288 in the lead-off spot. The great tools that Al Campanis had seen in the tryout at Sixto Escobar Stadium were gradually becoming polished to major-league quality.

"Roberto," said Pedrín Zorilla, "I have spoken with Mr. Campanis. The Dodgers would like to sign you to a contract with their Triple-A team in Montreal. They will pay you a signing bonus of $10,000 and a salary of $5,000 for the year."

Roberto sat on Señor Zorilla's patio and considered the offer. It seemed only a short time ago that Zorilla had offered him $400 to play for the Santurce Crabbers. Now they were speaking of thousands and a chance to play for the Brooklyn Dodgers.

Still, Roberto was not certain. During the last few months he had been approached by scouts from many major-league teams. The Dodgers' offer was excellent—$10,000 was an enormous sum for a Puerto Rican player. And yet, who could tell what the others might be willing to pay?

Ah, but the Dodgers! Roberto thought. They are the team of Jackie Robinson, the first black man in the major leagues. For the last two years they have won the pennant. They are the team of Duke Snider and Carl Furillo, the batting champion. No, he thought, the Dodgers are not like any other team. The Dodgers are special.

"Well, Roberto," asked Señor Zorilla, "what shall I tell them?"

Roberto looked seriously at Señor Zorilla. "Tell them I will sign," he said.

Señor Zorilla smiled and led Roberto into his wood-paneled study. "I will draw up a temporary agreement," he said, "and you can take it home to your father."

Roberto was full of excitement as he left Señor Zorilla's house. The Dodgers' Triple-A team in Montreal was only one short step away from the major leagues. He was on his way!

Later that day, however, his excitement turned to confusion. A scout from the Milwaukee Braves contacted Roberto and offered him a bonus of $28,000. Roberto grew dizzy when he thought of so much money. $10,000 was more money than he'd ever imagined. But $28,000—that was a fortune!

"What shall I do?" Roberto asked that evening as he sat with his mother and father. "I promised to go with the Dodgers, but we have not yet signed the agreement."

Don Melchor silently considered the situation, but it was Doña Luisa who finally spoke. "Momen," she said, "if you gave the word, you keep the word."

6

It's for Your Own Good

When Roberto Clemente joined the Montreal Royals in the spring of 1954, he felt very lonely and very far from home. Montreal is almost 2,000 miles north of Puerto Rico. The weather is cool, and there is snow on the distant mountains even in the summertime. Roberto missed his family and friends. He missed the warm Puerto Rican sun and the good meals of rice and beans and roast pork.

Most of the people in Montreal spoke French. The players on the Royals spoke English. So did the people in the other cities the Royals visited. Roberto thought back to his classes at Vizcarrondo High School in Carolina. It is one thing to study English in a book. It is something else to speak it. And as for French—that was even more mysterious. He was a stranger in a strange land.

But if Roberto was confused by the simple things

of everyday life, he was even more confused by the strange things that happened on the baseball field.

"Time!" Manager Max Macon stepped out of the Montreal dugout. It was the first inning of a game in Richmond, Virginia. Montreal had the bases loaded and Roberto Clemente was on his way to the plate. Macon called him back to the dugout and sent up a pinch hitter. Roberto stared at his manager in amazement.

"Why you do this?" he asked.

"Don't worry, son," said Macon, "it's for your own good."

As Roberto sat on the bench and watched the rest of the game, he tried to understand his manager's words. My own good, he thought. What good? The first week of the season I hit a long home run into the wind. The next day I am sitting on the bench. When the weather is cold and I am swinging badly, they tell me to play. Now it is a warm night, and I am ready to show them what I can do. He takes me out in the first inning with the bases loaded!

After the game, Roberto talked with Joe Black in their hotel. Black was a tall, powerfully built pitcher who had played in the Negro Leagues before becoming a star with the Brooklyn Dodgers. In 1953, his blazing fastball helped the Dodgers win the National League pennant. But now Black was having trouble with his arm, and the Dodgers had sent him to Montreal to get it back into shape.

"Why does he do this?" Roberto asked. "A pinch hitter in the first inning!"

Black smiled kindly at the younger man. "They're hiding you," he said. Black was one of the few players on the Royals who spoke Spanish, and he had quickly taken a liking to Roberto. "Hiding me?" said Roberto. "What do you mean? Who is he hiding me from?"

"From the other teams. They don't want anyone else to know how good you are."

"I don't understand."

"Look, Roberto. The Dodgers paid you a bonus, right?"

"Yes," said Roberto. "$10,000."

"Exactly. Now they've got a new bonus rule this year. It's kind of complicated, but it goes something like this: any player who gets $4,000 or more has to be on the roster of the major-league club. If they leave you off the roster, you can be drafted by another team at the end of the year."

Roberto thought about Black's words. "But it is stupid," he said. "If the Dodgers don't want me, why did they offer me a contract?" Black shook his head and smiled. "Oh, they want you all right," he said. "They just don't want you right now."

Roberto frowned in frustration and looked around the hotel room. The furniture was worn, and the faded wallpaper was slowly peeling away from the wall. A single bare light bulb hung from the ceiling. The night was hot, and Roberto could hear the shouts of people from the street below.

In the other cities that the Royals visited, all of the players stayed in the same hotel. But in Richmond, the black players stayed in a separate hotel in a separate part of town. They ate their meals in separate restaurants. They drank from separate drinking fountains. "I still do not understand why they won't let me play," said Roberto. "I think it is stupid. But this is more stupid. In Puerto Rico a black man can go anywhere. He can eat anywhere. He can talk to anyone. Even in Montreal, they treat us with respect. But here," he said, pointing around the small hotel room, "here we are second-class citizens."

Joe Black nodded sympathetically. "I know," he said. "Believe me, I know. But you can't let them get to you. Remember, this isn't Puerto Rico, and it isn't Montreal. This is Richmond, Virginia, Roberto. This is the South. A few years ago, a black man couldn't even play on that baseball field."

"I don't care," said Roberto. "I think it is childish."

As spring turned into summer, Roberto continued to be frustrated by the strange strategy of his manager. In one game, he hit three triples. The next day, he was sitting on the bench. If he struck out, he stayed in the game. If he got a hit, he was certain to be replaced.

When Al Campanis visited Montreal on one of his regular scouting trips, Roberto decided to speak up. Like Joe Black, Campanis spoke Spanish. Roberto felt comfortable talking with the man who had first discovered him at the tryout in Sixto Escobar Stadium.

"I want to go home, Mr. Campanis. I know I can play better than these guys, but they won't play me. The other night, we get five runs in the first inning, and they take me out. Mr. Macon does not like me."

Al Campanis looked at the young ballplayer. Roberto was almost twenty years old. He was 5′ 11″ tall and carried 175 pounds of solid muscle. Campanis knew that Roberto had all the tools to be a major-league player. But he also knew that the Brooklyn Dodgers had one of the finest outfields in the game.

The year before, right fielder Carl Furillo had

led the league with a .344 average. In center field, Duke Snider batted .336 and hit 42 home runs. In left field, Jackie Robinson batted .329. In 1954, there was no room on the Dodgers for Roberto Clemente. Brooklyn's only hope was to keep their young future star hidden in Montreal.

"Do you trust me?" Campanis asked.

"I trust you," said Roberto.

"Then believe me. Everything will turn out all right for Roberto Clemente."

Clyde Sukeforth sat in the stands at Parker Field in Richmond and watched the Montreal Royals practicing before the game. It was a hot, humid evening, and he tried to keep cool by fanning himself with his program. But Sukeforth quickly forgot the heat as he stared at a young outfielder wearing number 21. Standing in deep center field, the player fired perfect strikes to home plate. What an arm! thought Sukeforth. Who is that kid?

Clyde Sukeforth was a scout for the Pittsburgh Pirates. If the Brooklyn Dodgers had too many good players in the early fifties, the Pirates had the opposite problem. In 1954, they were on their way to their third consecutive season in the cellar. The only benefit of a last-place finish was the number-one pick in the draft.

Sukeforth had gone down to Richmond to take a look at Joe Black. The Pirates and Dodgers were discussing a possible trade for the veteran pitcher. But as soon as Sukeforth saw Roberto Clemente warming up in the outfield, the Pittsburgh scout forgot about Joe Black and concentrated his attention on the teenager from Puerto Rico.

Before the game began, Sukeforth went to a phone booth and called Branch Rickey, the Pirates' general manager. At the age of 73, Rickey was the grand old man of American baseball. During the 1930s, he put together the famous Gas House Gang in St. Louis. During the 1940s, he broke the color barrier and signed Jackie Robinson for the Brooklyn Dodgers. Now he was trying to rescue the Pittsburgh Pirates from the deep, dark basement of the National League.

"I tell you, Mr. Rickey," said Sukeforth, "this Clemente kid looks like the real thing. He's got an arm like a cannon."

"Can he hit?" asked Rickey.

"He looks good in batting practice."

"Is he available?"

"Definitely," said Sukeforth. "He's a bonus baby, but the Dodgers left him off the roster."

For a moment, Branch Rickey was silent on the other end of the phone. Only a few years earlier, he had sent Clyde Sukeforth to scout Jackie Robinson in the Negro Leagues. Together they had brought a great star to the Brooklyn Dodgers. Now they hoped to take one away. "Good," said Rickey finally. "Keep an eye on him, Clyde."

Sukeforth returned to his seat for the beginning of the game. As usual, Roberto sat in frustration on the Royals' bench, watching the other players take the field. Finally, late in the game, manager Max Macon sent Roberto to the plate as a pinch hitter. Clyde Sukeforth liked his swing, but the Pirates wanted to be sure.

Branch Rickey assigned another scout named Howie Haak to follow the Royals, hoping to see more of Roberto. It was like a game of cat and mouse. In two weeks, Haak only saw Clemente bat four times. Late in the season, Clyde Sukeforth went up to Montreal for one last look.

"I notice you haven't been playing Clemente much." Sukeforth smiled across the dinner table at Max Macon. The two men had known each other for years. There was no sense in their trying to fool each other. "Well, I don't care if you never play him," continued the Pittsburgh scout. "We're going to finish last, and we're going to draft him number one."

With that Sukeforth got up from the table. "Take care of our boy," he said.

On November 22, 1954, the Pittsburgh Pirates chose Roberto Clemente number one in the baseball draft. When Roberto heard the news, he was happy to be drafted by a team that really wanted him. After his frustrating season in Montreal, he looked forward to playing regularly. He was eager to show the fans what Roberto Clemente could do. There was only one thing that puzzled him. "Where is Pittsburgh?" he wondered.

I Play like Roberto Clemente

Roberto knelt in the on-deck circle and looked around the wide open spaces of Forbes Field. It was a warm, sunny day, and the green grass of the old ballpark seemed to stretch forever. It is beautiful, thought Roberto. Very beautiful. But so big! I will have to forget about hitting home runs.

Since 1909, Forbes Field had been the home of the Pittsburgh Pirates. It was the biggest park in the league. Down the left-field foul line the distance was 365 feet. From there, the ivy-covered brick wall angled to a point in left-center field that was an incredible 457 feet from home plate. For a right-handed hitter like Roberto, it was useless to try to pull the ball out of the park.

As Roberto stepped up to the plate, his heart beat quickly with excitement. There were over 20,000 people in the stands, and it seemed like every one of them was watching him. It was Sunday, April 17,

1955, and the Pittsburgh Pirates were playing the first game of a double-header against the Brooklyn Dodgers. For the Pirates, it was their first home game of the season after three straight losses on the road. For Roberto Clemente, it was his first time at bat in the major leagues.

On the mound for the Dodgers was a young left-hander named Johnny Podres. Roberto set his right foot deep in the batter's box and took his practice swings. As he cocked his bat and waited for the pitch, he felt a flash of anger. The Dodgers did not want me, he thought. Well, I will show them how Roberto Clemente plays baseball.

Podres went into his windup and delivered the pitch. With his short, compact swing, Roberto pounded a hard ground ball toward the hole between shortstop and third base. Roberto flew down the first base line as Dodger shortstop Pee Wee Reese ran to his right and stopped the ball with the tip of his glove. By the time that Reese recovered the ball and threw to first base, Roberto was safe with his first major-league hit.

The next day, the Pirates traveled to New York to play the Giants at the Polo Grounds. Before the game, Roberto stopped by the Giants' dugout to say hello to Willie Mays. That winter, Roberto and Mays had played together in the outfield of the Santurce Crabbers. Although he was only a few years older than Roberto, Mays was already a major-league superstar.

"Hey, Robby," said Mays. "Nice to see you."

"Hello, Willie," said Roberto.

"I hear you got a couple of hits against the Dodgers," said Mays. "That's good. You keep hittin' 'em all year."

Roberto laughed. At that time, the Dodgers and the Giants were the two powers of the National League. "Hey, Willie," he said with a smile, "I gonna hit the Giants, too."

Mays chuckled with delight. "I bet you will," he said. "I just bet you will." Mays continued to smile to himself for a moment. Then he looked at Roberto. "Listen, Robby," he said seriously, "don't let the pitchers here show you up. Get mean when you go to bat. If they try to knock you down, act like it doesn't bother you. Get up and hit the ball. Show 'em."

Willie Mays was not the only Giants player that Roberto knew from the Puerto Rican winter league. Playing beside Mays in the Giant outfield was Monte Irvin, Roberto's boyhood idol. As he returned to the Pirates' dugout, Roberto passed the muscular veteran waiting for his turn at batting practice.

"Hello, Mr. Irvin," said Roberto politely. Even now, it was hard for him to look his hero directly in the eye.

Irvin smiled and held out his hand to the younger man. "Monte," he said. "Just call me Monte."

During the first four innings, the Giants pounded the Pirate pitchers for eleven runs. When Roberto came to bat in the top of the fifth, the game was already out of reach. But a rookie is a rookie, no matter what the score. The Giant pitcher leaned back and fired a hard inside fastball that sent Roberto sprawling in the dirt.

As he got up from the ground, Roberto glared angrily out at the mound. But when he stepped back into the batter's box, he remembered Willie Mays' advice. Yes, he thought, I will show him in my own way.

On the next pitch, Roberto smashed a long drive to the gap in right-center field. The ball dropped between Mays and Monte Irvin and rolled toward the distant wall of the Polo Grounds. As the Giant outfielders chased after the ball, Roberto tore around the bases and slid across the plate with an inside-the-park home run.

After his first week in the major leagues, Roberto was batting .360. It was a brilliant start, but it didn't last. As the National League pitchers saw more of the younger player from Puerto Rico, they noticed that he bobbed his head at the plate and had trouble following the path of a slow curveball. They also noticed that he would swing at bad pitches. Roberto struck out more and more. And the Pirates continued to lose.

"That's twenty-two, Clemente."

Roberto looked up at his manager, Fred Haney. Haney was a small, balding man who had managed the Pirates through two miserable seasons and was in the middle of a third. "Twenty-two what?" asked Roberto.

"Batting helmets," said Haney. "Twenty-two batting helmets."

Roberto looked down at the concrete floor of the Pirate dugout. There at his feet were the shattered pieces of a black plastic batting helmet. When he was frustrated with himself or with the team, he took a bat and smashed his batting helmet to bits. It made him feel better for a little while.

Haney had tried to be patient. He knew it was hard to be a rookie in the big leagues. It was hard to play on a losing team. But enough was enough. "I don't mind you tearing up your own clothes," he said, "but if you're going to destroy club property, you're going to pay for it."

Roberto looked up at Haney. He was still angry. "How much?" he asked.

"Ten bucks apiece," said Haney.

Roberto looked down again at the pieces of plastic on the dugout floor. He did some quick arithmetic in his mind. Twenty-two helmets at $10.00 each was $220.00. For a rookie who was only making the minimum major-league salary of $6,000 a year, that was too much money to waste. "OK," he said quietly, "I stop breaking the hats."

Roberto stopped breaking batting helmets, but his anger continued. His problems with the National League pitchers were only a small part of the frustrations of his rookie year. Like Montreal, Pittsburgh was a strange city, very different from Barrio San Antón or the streets of San Juan. Most of the people were white factory workers. The black people lived in a separate section of the city called The Hill.

Early in the season, a Pirate pitcher named Bob Friend introduced Roberto to a black man named Phil Dorsey. Phil was eight years older than Roberto, and he did his best to help him get used to Pittsburgh. When Roberto had trouble sleeping in his hotel, Dorsey found him a room with a nice couple named Mr. and Mrs. Stanley Gardner. The

Gardners were white, but they treated Roberto like a son.

The players on the Pirates and the other teams of the National League were not so kind. In 1955, many white players still did not like the idea of playing with blacks. For Roberto, it was even harder. He was not only black. He was Puerto Rican. Even on his own team, some of the players made fun of him and called him "nigger." Roberto grew furious at their insults. In Puerto Rico, he thought, no one called another person "nigger."

There were other insults as well. In the newspapers, the writers called him a "Puerto Rican hot dog." When they quoted the things he said, they exaggerated his accent. "I no play so gut, yet," they would write. "Me like hot weather, veree hot. I no run fast cold weather." Roberto still had trouble with English, but he did not speak as poorly as the writers made him sound.

To make matters worse, Roberto had to sit out many games because of pain in his lower back. During the winter, a drunken driver had rammed into his car at sixty miles per hour. In his mind, Roberto could still hear the horrible explosion of metal and glass on the Puerto Rican highway. He could see the blood trickling down the other driver's face and smell the alcohol on the drunken man's breath. Worst of all, he could feel the wrenching pain in his lower back as the cars collided.

The doctors said there was nothing wrong, but ever since the accident, his back would get sore when he played too many games. Many of the sports-writers and the Pirate players did not believe he was really injured. They said he was "jaking it," baseball slang for pretending to be hurt.

More than anything else, Roberto wanted to play baseball. He could not believe that the players and writers would doubt his word. If he was not injured, why would he want to sit on the bench? The more he thought about it, the more he was sure that the only reason they doubted him was because he was black and did not speak their language.

"I don't believe in color," Roberto said. "I believe in people. I always respect everyone, and thanks to God my mother and my father taught me never to hate, never to dislike someone because of their color. I didn't even know about this stuff when I got here."

There were two other black players on the Pirates that season, Curt Roberts, an infielder from Oakland, California, and Román Mejías, a young outfielder from Cuba. Roberts, a second-year player, told Clemente, "Keep your mouth shut. You can't change anything."

"I don't care," said Roberto angrily. "I don't want to be put down because I am Puerto Rican. I don't stand for disliking people because of their color. If that is the case, then I don't want to be living. I am a double nigger . . . for my skin *and* my heritage."

"Mr. Clemente! Mr. Clemente! Can I have your autograph?"

"Hey, Roberto! Gimme your autograph!"

"Clemente! Clemente!"

Roberto looked at the crowd of boys and girls waiting outside the players' entrance at Forbes Field. It was like this after every Pirate game. Many of the players did not like signing autographs. They would scribble their names quickly on a few scorecards and move on. They had families and friends and places to go. But Roberto was in no hurry. He would stand for hours, signing autographs and talking with the fans.

"Roberto! Roberto!"

"Me first!"

"C'mon, Clemente!"

"Take it easy," Roberto said with a smile. "I gonna sign for everybody."

As he reached for a scorecard and began to sign

his name, Roberto felt good inside. These are the ones who really matter, he thought. The children. They do not care about black or white. They are in love with baseball.

Two hours later, the crowd of children had disappeared. Roberto looked down at a ten-year-old girl waiting patiently in her wheelchair. Her mother stood behind her. "Please, Mr. Clemente," the girl said, "will you sign my scorecard?"

Roberto squatted down so he could look her in the eye.

"What's your name?" he asked.

"Ellen," said the girl.

"Hey, Ellen," Roberto asked, "how come you wait so long?"

Ellen blushed and smiled. "That's OK," she said. "You're my favorite player."

"It's true, Mr. Clemente," said her mother. "She checks the paper every day to see how you do."

Roberto frowned as if he were in pain. "Oooh," he said. "I am sorry. I don't play so good right now."

"Don't worry," said Ellen seriously. "You'll come around. Just be careful with those outside curveballs."

Roberto laughed. "Yeah, that's what my manager always says."

Roberto took the scorecard and signed his autograph. When he was finished, he looked at the girl's mother. "Where's your car?" he asked. "I give Ellen a push."

"Thank you very much, Mr. Clemente, but that won't be necessary."

"You sure?"

The woman smiled uncomfortably. "Yes, well, actually, you see, we don't have a car. We came on the bus."

Roberto frowned. "But the buses go right after the game. How you gonna get home?"

"We'll be all right. We can get a cab."

Roberto thought for a moment. "No," he said, "you miss the bus because you wait for me. I gonna drive you home."

"Oh no," the woman said. "We couldn't ask you to do that. It's thirty miles."

"That's OK," said Roberto. "I got nothing else to do. Besides, I gotta be nice to Ellen. Maybe someday she gonna be a batting coach."

Roberto continued to struggle at the plate throughout this rookie season, finally finishing with a .255 average. It was respectable, especially on the lowly Pirates, but it was nothing special. In the outfield, however, he quickly established himself as an outstanding performer. It was a combination of natural ability and hard work.

The right-field wall at Forbes Field was a challenge for any player. From the foul line, it angled sharply to straightaway right and then angled again to right center. Roberto would have the other Pirate players smash line drives off the wall as he spent hours and hours practicing the tricky bounces.

When the Pirates went on the road, he would inspect the right-field area of the opponent's ball park to see the height of the grass and the angles of the wall. When it rained, he would come to the park early and practice picking up the wet ball.

"I knew if I could not play right field well," Roberto said, "I might not play regularly. I didn't like that much."

Late in the 1955 season, the last-place Pirates once again played the Giants at the Polo Grounds. After the final game of the series, Roberto was interviewed on the radio.

"Roberto," the announcer said, "you had a fine day and a fine series here. As a young fellow starting out, you remind me of another rookie outfielder who could run, throw, and get those clutch hits. Young fellow of ours, name of Willie Mays."

To the announcer, this was a great compliment. Willie Mays was one of the finest players in the game of baseball. But Roberto did not like to be compared to another player, no matter how great he was. For a moment, Roberto was silent, carefully considering the correct English words.

"Nonetheless," he said, "I play like Roberto Clemente."

8

I Will Try It One More Year

Roberto leaned over his mother's shoulder and smelled the chicken and rice cooking on the stove. "Oh, Mamá," he said, "that smells so good."

Doña Luisa smiled and continued to stir the big pot of food. "Momen," she said, "you look so skinny. Don't they feed you in Pittsburgh?"

"Sure they feed me," Roberto said. "I eat steak every night."

Don Melchor sat at the table, listening to their conversation. "Every night?" he said. "How can you afford steak every night?"

"Well, not every night," Roberto said seriously. "Besides, when we're on the road, the team gives me money for meals."

Don Melchor nodded. "That's good," he said. "You need the red meat for strength."

Roberto sat down and joined his father at the table as Doña Luisa dished out heaping portions of food. It was good to be back home with his family, he thought. It was good to hear his own language. Once again he was playing for the Santurce Crabbers. In the winter league he was an established star. When he rested for a game or two, no one accused him of "jaking it."

"Papá," he said. "Mamá. There is something I want to discuss. Last year, I missed many games because of my back. When I did play, I could not play my best. What is the point in playing if I cannot do my best?"

Don Melchor and Doña Luisa sat quietly, thinking about Roberto's question. Finally, Doña Luisa spoke. "Perhaps you should go back to school, Momen. Then you will have something else if you cannot play baseball."

"But, Mamá," Roberto said, "baseball is my life."

"Tell me, Momen," said Don Melchor, "what do the doctors say?"

Roberto frowned. "They do not know. They cannot find anything wrong. Many people in Pittsburgh think I am pretending. But they do not have to play in pain. I tell you it is there. I feel it."

"How is it since you are home?" asked Doña Luisa.

Roberto smiled. "It's a little better, Mamá. Here

the weather is warmer, and we don't travel so far to play. I can sleep in my own bed and eat your good food."

"Momen," said Don Melchor, "you are a man now. Your mother and I cannot tell you what to do. You must make the decision."

Roberto slowly chewed his food as he thought to himself. He was very disappointed in his first year at Pittsburgh. He knew he could play much better. When he did not play well, he felt that he was cheating the fans. Even if some of the other players called him names and the writers made fun of him in the papers, the fans were his friends. Yes, he thought, the fans of the Pittsburgh Pirates deserve to see Roberto Clemente at his best.

"I will try it one more year," he said. "If I still hurt, then I quit."

When a team finishes last for four straight years, something has to change. After the 1955 season, Branch Rickey retired as general manager of the Pirates and became the club president. The new general manager was Joe L. Brown. As one of his first actions, Brown hired a new field manager, Bobby Bragan.

In May, the Pirates obtained a talented center fielder named Bill Virdon in a trade with the St.

Louis Cardinals. At second base, they brought up a brilliant fielder by the name of Bill Mazeroski from the minor leagues. With Roberto in right field, Frank Thomas at third base, Dick Groat at shortstop, and a slugger named Dale Long at first, the Pirates suddenly had a solid group of players.

The changes were good for Roberto as well as for the team. He felt comfortable with Long and Virdon and Mazeroski. It did not seem to matter so much who was black or who was white. It did not matter if his English was not so good. They were just young ballplayers who wanted to win.

At first the Pirates did exactly that. With Bob Friend pitching well and Clemente, Virdon, and Long hitting consistently, the Pittsburgh Pirates took first place in the National League on June 13. After four seasons of watching their team in the cellar, the Pirate fans were overjoyed.

It didn't last. A few days later, the Pirates began to slide back toward the bottom of the pack. But even as the team returned to its losing ways, Roberto gave the Pittsburgh fans something to cheer about.

Roberto stepped to the plate in the bottom of the ninth. It was a warm, humid evening in late July. His muscles felt loose and ready. The Pirates were down 8–5, but the bases were loaded with nobody out. On the mound for the Cubs was Jim Brosnan, a tall right-hander with a good fastball and a better slider.

Roberto looked down at his manager, Bobby Bragan, who was coaching at third base. Earlier in the season, Roberto had missed a signal to bunt in a close game and Bragan had fined him $25.00. But this time there was no bunt sign. There was nothing to do but swing away.

Brosnan leaned back and fired. Roberto whipped his bat around and smashed a long fly to left center, the deepest part of Forbes Field. As Roberto's long drive bounced in the outfield grass and rolled toward the distant fence, the three Pirate runners raced around to score.

Roberto followed behind them, his legs churning at full speed. As he approached third base, Bobby Bragan held up his hands. "Stop!" he shouted. The game was tied and the Cub center fielder already had the ball. There was no sense in taking a chance.

"Get out of my way!" Roberto screamed. Never hesitating, he rounded third and headed for home. The throw from center field reached the plate at the same time as the speeding runner. Roberto slid under the catcher's tag and scored the winning run with an inside-the-park grand slam!

After the game, the local sportswriters crowded

around Roberto in the Pirate locker room. His daring play was against all the rules of baseball logic. With the game tied and nobody out, it would have been much safer to stop at third and wait to score. But Roberto had a logic of his own.

"I think we got nothing to lose," he said. "We got the score tied without my run, and if I score the game is over and we don't have to play no more tonight."

After talking with Roberto, the reporters interviewed Bobby Bragan in his office. "Are you going to fine Clemente for running through your sign?" asked one of the writers.

Bragan leaned back in his chair and smiled. "Roberto is quite a player," he said. "He just likes to hit and run."

By the end of the 1956 season, the Pirates were in seventh place. Although it was a disappointing finish, at least it was a slight improvement. At least it was not last.

For Roberto, the season was more than a slight improvement. He batted .311, the third-highest average in the National League. In the field, he was spectacular, gunning down twenty base runners with his powerful arm. On a single to right, he would watch the hitter out of the corner of his eye as he rounded first base. If the player went too far beyond the bag, Roberto fired the ball to first baseman Dale Long and suddenly the hit was an out.

There was no more talk of quitting or "jaking it." Throughout the long season, Roberto only missed seven games because of his back. He played hard and he played well. Roberto Clemente was in the big leagues to stay.

That winter, Roberto received a big raise in his salary from the Pirates. He used some of the money to buy a new home for his parents. Roberto was proud that he could help Don Melchor and Doña Luisa. "I do not think I am giving my parents something," he said. "I am trying to pay them back for giving me so much."

His back was improving along with his bank book. He hit .396 in the winter league, and he looked forward to his third major-league season. But then disaster struck. Early in spring training, Roberto reinjured his back. He had to sit out the first two games of the season and spent most of the year playing with a back brace.

The Pirates also struggled, along with Roberto. In August, Bobby Bragan was fired as manager and replaced by Danny Murtaugh. Murtaugh was a former second baseman for the Pirates who demanded a lot from his players. During the rest of the season, the Pirates won as many games as they lost, but they still finished in a tie for last place.

Both Roberto and the Pirates were healthier in 1958. It was the team's first full season under Murtaugh, and they were in the middle of an exciting pennant race all year. They finally finished in second place behind the Milwaukee Braves, but they won more games than any Pirate team in the last twenty years.

Many people in Pittsburgh thought the Pirates had a chance to win the pennant in 1959. Roberto was also ready for a good year. He spent the winter in the Marine Corps Reserve, and the hard training helped to strengthen his back. But then, on May 17, he was hit on the right elbow by a pitch. A week later he was placed on the disabled list for forty days. This meant he could not play in a game, even for an inning.

It was very frustrating for Roberto to sit on the bench day after day and watch the other players trying to win. Danny Murtaugh was also frustrated. The Pirate manager was a tough Irishman who believed that a player should keep on playing no matter how badly he was hurt. One day in the Pirate dugout, Murtaugh looked angrily at Roberto. "You're faking the injury," Murtaugh said. "Take off the uniform."

Roberto stared back at his manager. He could feel the blood rushing to his face. How could anyone think he would want to sit on the bench? "No one takes off my uniform while I am playing for the Pirates," Roberto said.

As he flew back to Puerto Rico at the end of the 1959 season, Roberto thought about his career. During five years in the major leagues, he had missed over 130 games because of injuries. When he was healthy, he played well, but he knew he could do better. His career batting average was .282. He averaged 47 RBI, 22 doubles, 8 triples, and 5 home runs per year. Only once had he batted over .300 or driven in more than 50 runs.

Many players would be happy with these solid statistics, but Roberto wanted to be more than a solid player. He wanted to be the best player he could possibly be. He wanted to be great—not only for himself, but for the people of Puerto Rico and the fans of Pittsburgh.

9

Beat 'Em, Bucs!

Ring! Ring! Ring!

Bob Campbell, head of the Pirate ticket office, picked up the phone. "Pittsburgh Pirates," he said.

"What tickets do you have left for Saturday?"

"We've got some seats in right field."

"Where's right field?"

"Behind Clemente," Campbell said.

"Oh," said the voice on the other end of the line, "that will be fine."

It was 1960 and the Pittsburgh Pirates were on top of the National League. Suddenly many new fans were coming to Forbes Field. Some of them didn't know much about baseball, but they knew about Roberto Clemente.

In May, while the Pirates were fighting the San Francisco Giants for first place, Roberto drove in 25 runs in 27 games. By the end of the month, he was leading the league with a batting average of

7 1

.353 and the Pirates were ahead of the Giants by one and a half games. Fans crowded into Forbes Field screaming, "Beat 'em, Bucs!" Bucs was short for Buccaneers, another name for the Pirates.

Throughout the season, Roberto's batting average never fell below .300. The Pirates were almost as consistent. They never lost more than four games in a row, and they could never be counted out of a game. Twenty-one times, the Bucs scored the winning run in the ninth inning.

During one eleven-game winning streak, Roberto wore the same T-shirt every day for good luck. As the Pirates kept winning, the other players on the team began to notice a strange smell. But nobody wanted him to change his shirt.

Roberto stood in right field, ready for action. It was a hot night in early August and the Pirates were playing the Giants at Forbes Field. For the last ten days, the Pirates had been in first place, slowly pulling away from the Milwaukee Braves. But there were still two months left in the season, and every game was important. As Willie Mays stepped to the plate in the top of the seventh inning, the Pirates were holding on to a 1–0 lead.

On the mound, the Pirate pitcher leaned back and delivered the pitch. Mays reached out and smashed a hard line drive down the right-field line. Roberto turned his back on the field and ran at full speed toward the right-field wall. I must catch it, he thought. I must catch it. At the last moment, he dove head first into the hard concrete wall.

The Pittsburgh fans stared in horror as Roberto slowly got up to his feet. There was blood gushing out of his chin and his knees were wobbly. He steadied himself for a moment. Then he lifted his left hand to show the crowd his glove. The stadium exploded with applause. He had caught the ball.

Roberto was rushed to the hospital in an ambulance. The doctors stitched up his jaw and he sat out the next five games waiting for it to heal. Without Roberto in the lineup, the Pirates' lead over Milwaukee slipped from seven games to two. But on Roberto's second day back, the Bucs beat the St. Louis Cardinals 4–1. Roberto drove in all four runs.

Throughout the rest of August and September, the Pirates held on to first place in the National League. It wasn't easy. They fought off the challenge of the Braves, only to find the Cardinals hot on their trail. On Sunday, September 25, the Pirates were playing the Braves in Milwaukee while the Cardinals were playing the Cubs. Either a victory by the Pirates or a loss by the Cardinals would give Pittsburgh its first pennant in 33 years.

Roberto knelt in the on-deck circle, waiting to bat against Warren Spahn, the great Milwaukee pitcher. Suddenly he heard screaming and yelling in the Pirate dugout. The Cubs had just beaten the Cardinals 5–0. Roberto looked at Dick Stuart, a young power-hitting first baseman who was waiting to bat after Roberto. "We win it?" Roberto asked. Stuart just nodded and smiled.

His heart beating with excitement, Roberto stepped up to the plate and smashed a line-drive single to center field. As he stood on first base, he looked over at the Pirate dugout and watched the players congratulating each other. This is why we play baseball, he thought. This is what we work for.

A few moments later, catcher Hal Smith pounded the ball for a double. Roberto rounded second at full speed and headed for third. The Pirate third-base coach held up his hands for Roberto to stop, but he ignored the sign and headed for home. Just as the ball arrived at the plate, Roberto scored in a cloud of dust.

After the game, a reporter asked Roberto why he ran through the coach's sign. Roberto looked at him as if he were crazy. "Stop at third?" he said. "I want to get to the bench quick and talk about winning the pennant."

It was a warm, hazy October afternoon as 36,683 fans crowded into Forbes Field to watch their Bucs take on the New York Yankees in the seventh game of the World Series. Many people were surprised that the Pirates had lasted so long against the powerful Yankees. In twelve years under manager Casey Stengel, the Bronx Bombers had won ten American League pennants and eight World Series. They had finished the regular season with fifteen straight victories, and they were expected to keep on rolling over the Pirates.

During the first six games, the Yankees pounded out 78 hits, including three long home runs by Mickey Mantle. They outscored the Pirates by a total of 46–17. But while the Yankees embarrassed the Pirates by scores of 16–3, 10–0, and 12–0, the Pirates managed to win the closer games. As Vernon Law took the mound for the Pirates in Game 7, the Series was tied at three games each.

Law had been the Pirates' star pitcher all season. He had already won two games in the Series, and when the Pirates scored four runs in the first two innings, it looked like Pittsburgh was on its way to the World Championship. But in the fifth and sixth innings, the Yankee bats suddenly came to life, pounding Law and ace reliever ElRoy Face as if they were pitching batting practice.

When the Pirates came to bat in the bottom of the eighth, they were behind 7–4. The fans in Forbes Field sat quietly in their seats. Their dreams of a World Championship were quickly disappearing.

With no outs and a man on first, Bill Virdon hit a hard ground ball to Yankee shortstop Tony Kubek. It looked like a sure double play, but something very strange happened. The ball suddenly hit a pebble in the infield and took an unexpected high bounce, striking Kubek in the throat. The Yankee shortstop was removed from the game and taken to the hospital. The Pirates had men on first and second with nobody out.

Dick Groat then smashed a single to left field, scoring the runner from second. The score was 7–5. The next two hitters were set down easily, but the runners moved to second and third. There were two outs, two men on, and the Pirates were still behind by two runs as Roberto stepped to the plate.

Roberto had played steadily throughout the Series. He was the only hitter on either team with at least one hit in each of the first six games. But so far in Game 7, the Yankee pitchers had held him hitless. Well, he thought as he cocked his bat and waited for the pitch, this is the time to start hitting.

A solid single would tie the game. A home run would put the Pirates ahead.

On the mound, Yankee pitcher Jim Coates looked at Roberto, crouched and ready at the plate. Keep it outside, Coates thought to himself. He'll swing at anything. Coates fired the first pitch a foot outside the plate. Roberto reached out and fouled it off for strike one. The next two pitches were also outside, and Roberto fouled them off as well. The count was no balls, two strikes. Coates had Clemente exactly where he wanted him.

On the fourth pitch, Roberto chopped a high bouncer past the mound and toward first base. As Roberto tore down the baseline, Yankee first baseman Bill Skowron moved to his right and fielded the ball. Jim Coates ran from the mound to cover first base. It looked like an easy out and the end of the inning for the Pirates. But Roberto beat Coates to the bag for an infield single. Virdon scored and Groat moved over to third. The Pirates were still alive.

Roberto stood at first base, catching his breath. There are many ways to win a baseball game, he thought. If you don't hit, you have to run.

The next batter was Hal Smith. On the mound, Jim Coates was shaken by Roberto's infield hit. He got two balls and two strikes on Smith. Then he leaned back and fired a fastball right over the heart of the plate. Smith smashed it into the left-field stands for a three-run homer.

The fans in Forbes Field went wild. Dick Groat trotted in from third and danced on home plate. Roberto, following behind him, bounced up and down the third base line like a happy kangaroo and scored in a jump of joy. Finally, Hal Smith rounded third and headed for home. As he crossed the plate, Roberto put his arms around the husky catcher and lifted him high in the air.

The Bucs had done it again! All year long they had come from behind to win in the late innings. Now, in the seventh game of the World Series, they had scored five runs in the eighth inning to take a 9–7 lead. As the Yankees came to bat in the top of the ninth, the old ballpark still rumbled with the noise of the crowd. Only three outs separated the Pittsburgh Pirates from the World Championship.

But the Yankees refused to give up, scoring twice to tie the game at 9–9. Once again the Pittsburgh fans grew very quiet. The first batter for the Pirates in the bottom of the ninth was second baseman Bill Mazeroski. On the mound for the Yankees was a young right-hander named Ralph Terry.

Mazeroski watched Terry's first pitch speed by

for ball one. On the second pitch, Terry leaned back and fired a high, hard fastball. Mazeroski whipped his bat around and smashed a long drive toward left field. Yankee outfielder Yogi Berra turned and watched helplessly as the ball sailed over his head and cleared the brick wall above the 406-foot mark.

As he rounded first base, Mazeroski jumped high in the air, ripped off his plastic batting helmet, and started swinging his right arm around and around like a windmill. The other Pirate players exploded out of the dugout and the Pittsburgh fans poured down from the stands to celebrate on the field. By the time Mazeroski got to home plate, he had to fight through hundreds of fans to score the winning run. As the Pirates rushed into the clubhouse, one fan took out a shovel and began to dig up home plate.

For the next twelve hours, the people of Pittsburgh celebrated as they had never celebrated before. They danced through the streets, shouting and screaming and singing. They blasted their car horns and tossed confetti from their office windows. They stopped traffic and turned the downtown area into one gigantic party. Their beloved Bucs, the team that didn't have a chance to win, had defeated the powerful Yankees in one of the strangest World Series in history.

In the Pirate clubhouse, the players poured champagne on each other and sprayed the mayor of Pittsburgh with beer. Roberto was just as happy as the others, but he had a different way of celebrating. He dressed quietly and congratulated his teammates on the victory. Then he left the Pirate clubhouse and walked out into the streets of Pittsburgh.

For hours, Roberto wandered among the people, sharing their joy, hugging them, congratulating them. These were the people who paid his salary. These were the people who believed in him when times were hard. Now he wanted to join them in celebrating the Pirates' victory.

Years later, Roberto remembered, "The biggest thrill was when I come out of the clubhouse after the last Series game and saw all those thousands of fans in the street. It was something you cannot describe. I did not feel like a player at the time. I feel like one of those persons, and I walked the streets among them."

10

Arriba!

At the end of the season, the baseball writers vote for the Most Valuable Player in each league. The MVP is a very special award. It does not always go to the man who has the highest batting average or hits the most home runs. It is awarded to the player who the writers feel has contributed the most to his team's success.

Usually, the MVP trophy is awarded to a player on the team that wins the pennant. In November of 1960, Roberto was at his parents' home in Puerto Rico when the results of the MVP voting were announced. The winner was Dick Groat, the Pirates' shortstop.

Roberto was very disappointed. Groat had led the league in batting with a .335 average. He was an excellent fielder and a team leader, but he had only driven in 50 runs. Roberto was third in the league with a .314 average, and he had driven in

94 runs, the highest total on the Pirates. For the last month of the season, while Groat was out of the lineup with a sprained wrist, Roberto had played hard every day.

As he looked down the list of other players in the MVP voting, Roberto became more and more angry. Don Hoak, the Pirates' third baseman, was second. Hoak was a tough competitor and a good fielder, but he did not hit like Roberto. After Hoak came Willie Mays of the Giants, Ernie Banks of the Cubs, Lindy McDaniel and Ken Boyer of the Cardinals, Pirate pitcher Vernon Law, and finally, in eighth place, Roberto Clemente.

Roberto was furious. After the finest season of his baseball career, he had not received a single first-place vote. The writers do not like me, he thought. They do not respect me because I am black and Puerto Rican. He thought back to the World Series. Even there, when I was the only player to get a hit in every game, you had to use a magnifying glass to find my name in the papers.

That evening, Roberto sat with his parents in the kitchen of their new home. It was much more modern than their old kitchen in Barrio San Antón. But his mother's cooking was just as delicious.

"This is wonderful, Mamá," Roberto said. "I really know I am home when I taste your roast pork."

Doña Luisa smiled and nodded toward the stove. "Eat, Momen," she said; "there's more when you're ready."

As Roberto ate hungrily, Don Melchor and Doña Luisa watched with pleasure. Roberto was no longer a boy. He was 26 years old, and a successful man of the world. But when he came home for the winter, he was still their Momen.

"I have been thinking," said Roberto. "Maybe Groat *was* most valuable. I don't know. But for me to be eighth! That is ridiculous. It is an insult. To me, to our island, and to our people."

Don Melchor nodded his head slowly, considering Roberto's words. "Momen," he said, "life is difficult. It is not always fair. But a man must keep on working."

"Yes, Papá," Roberto replied. "A man must keep on working." For a moment, Roberto sat silently, thinking to himself. Then he looked at his parents and spoke. His voice was very serious. "This year I had the best season of my career. But I will do better. Papá, Mamá, I make you a solemn promise. I will become the best hitter in baseball."

George Sisler watched Roberto in the batting cage at the Pirates' spring training camp in Fort Meyers, Florida. Sisler was the Pirate batting coach, and he was a man who knew how to hit. In 1920, he set the major-league record for most hits in one season with 257. That year, he led the American League with a batting average of .407. Two years later, he repeated as batting champion with a .420 average.

Ever since Roberto had joined the Pirates in 1955, Sisler had worked with him on his hitting. Unlike most great hitters, Roberto stood deep in the batter's box and far away from the plate. He liked to step into the pitch. If the ball was outside, he simply took a longer stride. George Sisler did not try to change Roberto's natural style. Instead, he concentrated on making the young player more patient at the plate.

"Hit only those pitches you like," Sisler told him. But Roberto had trouble waiting for the right pitch. He liked them all.

In 1960, however, Roberto had walked 39 times. He still swung at many bad pitches, but it was an improvement. Now, in the spring of 1961, he made another improvement. He began using a heavier bat to slow down his swing and make better contact with the ball.

Sisler smiled as he watched Roberto smash hard line drives all over the field. When Roberto was finished, the coach took him aside. "You look good in there, Bob," he said. "If you can stay away from the bad pitches, I think you can win the batting title this year."

Roberto raised his eyebrows as if he were surprised at the prediction. But inside he was confident. Of course I can win the batting title, he thought.

"Arriba! Arriba!" The fans in Forbes Field shouted joyfully as Roberto came to the plate. "Arriba" is a Spanish word that means, "Let's go!" A few years earlier, a Pirate announcer named Bob Prince had started yelling "Arriba!" when Roberto came to bat or made a great play in right field. In 1961, the cry of "Arriba!" caught fire with the Pittsburgh fans.

Roberto caught fire with the bat. On June 30, he was selected as the starting right fielder for the National League All-Star team. The year before, he had played in the All-Star game as a back-up player, but this was the first time he had been voted to the starting team.

When Roberto heard the news, he felt very proud. It is the writers who choose the MVP, he thought, but it is the players who choose the All-Stars. In the next nine days, Roberto hit even better than before. In a game against the Chicago Cubs, he got five hits in five at-bats, drove in five runs, and scored four. Two days later, he got four hits in four at-bats against Milwaukee. By the All-Star game, Roberto was the top batter in the National League with a batting average of .357.

Candlestick Park in San Francisco is famous for its cold, windy weather. But the afternoon was hot and windless as the National League All-Stars took the field on July 11, 1961.

Roberto looked around at his teammates. Out of the 25 players on the National League team, nine were black. They included great stars like Willie Mays, Henry Aaron, and Frank Robinson. In left field was Orlando Cepeda, another player from Puerto Rico. Of course there were also great white players like Warren Spahn, Stan Musial, and Sandy Koufax.

This is the way it should be, Roberto thought, blacks and whites playing together. The skin color is not important. It is only the man that matters.

In the second inning, Roberto pounded a long line drive to the fence in right-center field. As Mickey Mantle and Roger Maris chased after the ball, he sped around the base paths and wound up at third with a triple. When the next batter hit a fly ball to Mantle, Roberto tagged third and raced home with the first run of the game. Two innings later, he drove in the second run of the game with a sacrifice fly to right.

At the end of eight innings, the National League

led by a score of 3–1. Suddenly, a cold, powerful wind began to blow in from San Francisco Bay. As the wind grew stronger, the game became sloppier and sloppier. In the top of the ninth, the National League players made three errors. Stu Miller, a tiny pitcher for the Giants, was actually blown off the mound. In the wild windstorm, the American League scored two runs to tie the game.

The wind continued to blow as the game went into extra innings. In the top of the tenth, the American League took the lead 4–3 on another National League error. As they came to bat in the bottom of the tenth, Roberto and his teammates had one last chance to save the game.

Henry Aaron, the great slugger of the Milwaukee Braves, led off with a pinch-hit single to center field. On the mound for the American League was a knuckleball pitcher named Hoyt Wilhelm. A knuckleball does not spin like other pitches. It darts and dances slowly in the air. Even on a still day, it is hard to control a knuckleball, but in the windstorm of Candlestick Park it was almost impossible.

With Willie Mays at the plate, one of Wilhelm's knucklers got past the catcher, and Aaron took second. Mays then smashed a double down the third base line, and Aaron scored the tying run. The next batter was Frank Robinson of the Cincinnati Reds. Again Wilhelm's knuckler went out of control, and Robinson was hit by a pitch.

Now it was up to Roberto. He stepped deep into the batter's box, cocked his bat, and waited for the pitch. Wilhelm's knuckleball danced in the wind like a puppet on a string. Roberto watched the ball until it was almost over the plate. Then he brought his bat around and smashed a line drive to right field. As Roberto raced for first, Willie Mays rounded third and headed for home. The National League had won by a score of 5–4!

After the game, the sportswriters surrounded Willie Mays, asking him about his big double in the tenth inning and how he scored the winning run. Mays pointed to Roberto, who was sitting a few feet away. "I didn't do it," Mays said. "This man next to me did it. Talk to him." Still, the reporters ignored Roberto.

But even though he was frustrated by the writers, Roberto knew he had played a great game. He had driven in the game-winning run, scored the first run, and driven in the second. He had proven to himself, to the players, and to the fans that Roberto Clemente deserved to be an All-Star.

But there was something else that made Roberto

feel even better. The National League manager was Danny Murtaugh of the Pirates. Usually, the All-Star manager substitutes for the starting players in the middle of the game. But Murtaugh had let Roberto play from start to finish, even with the great Henry Aaron on the bench.

"What makes me feel most good," Roberto said, "is that Danny Murtaugh let me play the whole game. He pay me a big compliment. I do not think I let him down."

At the end of the 1961 season, Roberto was the batting champion of the National League with an average of .351. He had 201 hits, including 23 home runs, 30 doubles, and 10 triples. He drove in 89 runs and scored 100. In the field, he led the league by throwing out 27 base runners.

The award for the batting championship is called the Silver Bat. There is another award called the Gold Glove, which is given to the best fielder at each position. In 1961, Roberto received his first Gold Glove Award as the best right fielder in the National League.

In October, Roberto and Orlando Cepeda flew back to Puerto Rico together. Cepeda, who was from the city of Ponce, had led the National League in home runs and runs batted in. Never before had any Puerto Rican player won a major hitting title. Now there were two of them in the same year!

As the plane flew into the San Juan airport, Roberto looked out over the city. It had changed since he was a boy. It was no longer a poor city of old run-down buildings. Now there were tall sky-scrapers and modern highways. He smiled to himself. We are both on the way up, he thought, Puerto Rico and Roberto Clemente.

When the plane landed, Roberto and Orlando received a hero's welcome. Eighteen thousand people stood cheering on the side of the road as they were driven from the airport to Sixto Escobar Stadium. Inside the stadium, Roberto looked around at the thousands of Puerto Ricans who had come to honor him. It seemed like only a few years since he had peeked through the fence to watch his hero Monte Irvin. Now it was Roberto Clemente they came to see.

He felt warm inside as he listened to their cheers. He was proud of what he had accomplished. But he was even prouder that he and Orlando could bring their honors home to the people of Puerto Rico.

11

It Is My Life

Oscar Landrau's drugstore is on the great plaza in the center of Carolina. On another corner of the plaza is the church of San Fernando, one of the oldest and most beautiful Catholic churches in Puerto Rico. One evening in January of 1964, Roberto walked into the drugstore to pick up some medicine. He didn't know it at the time, but less than a year later, he'd be walking down the aisle on the other side of the plaza.

Señor Landrau had to leave on an errand, so Roberto picked up a newspaper and sat down to wait. He was all alone in the store. After a few minutes, the door opened and another customer walked in. Roberto looked up from his paper and felt his heart beating quickly. Standing just inside the door was a young woman in her early twenties. She was tall and graceful with intelligent eyes and striking, delicate features. Roberto thought she was the most beautiful girl he had ever seen.

The girl looked around the store and saw that the pharmacist was not in. Then she glanced nervously at Roberto and turned to leave. It was not proper for a well-bred Puerto Rican girl to be alone with a man she did not know.

"Don't leave," Roberto said. "Oscar will be back in a few minutes." Roberto smiled, trying to put her at ease. "How come I've never seen you before?" he asked. "Are you from Carolina?"

"Yes, sir," the girl replied.

"What is your name?"

"Vera."

"What is your last name?"

"Zabala."

"Hmmm," said Roberto. "Are you related to Rafael Zabala who plays for the team in Arecibo?"

"He's a distant relation," Vera replied. "I've never met him."

Just then, the pharmacist returned. Vera picked up her order and left. Roberto watched her as she walked out the door and into the plaza. "Tell me, Oscar," he said. "What do you know about this girl?"

"Ah, my friend," said the pharmacist, "her father is very strict. He raises his girls the old-fashioned way. You won't see her too often in the streets."

"Well then," said Roberto, "I will just have to find another way."

During the next few days, Roberto did some detective work. He discovered that a distant relative of his named Mercedes lived on the same street as the Zabala family. Through Mercedes, he arranged to take Vera to a baseball game. Of course, he could not be alone with her on the first date. Mercedes, her two sons, and Roberto's nephew all came along as chaperones.

Vera had never been to a baseball game. She had heard games on the radio, and she knew that Roberto was a big star. But as they drove from Carolina to the stadium in San Juan, she was looking forward to seeing the game in person. Roberto was very excited, too. After all, baseball was his life. He could think of no better way to impress Vera than to show her the way he played.

It was a perfect plan except for one minor detail: the game was rained out. Roberto tried to make the best of it by inviting Vera to dinner. Everyone else thought that was a good idea, but Vera refused. "My father gave me permission to go to the game," she said, "not to go to dinner."

A few days later, Roberto called Vera at the

bank where she worked and invited her to lunch. "No, thank you," she said. "Maybe some other time."

Roberto refused to give up. It's like a baseball game, he thought. If you're striking out, you have to adjust your batting style. He asked his niece to invite Vera to lunch. This time Vera accepted, and the niece told her many wonderful things about Roberto. The next time Roberto called, Vera agreed to join him for dinner. By the time Roberto left for spring training, he and Vera were engaged to be married.

Even while he was falling in love, Roberto continued to practice his hitting. Sometimes he would take a sack full of bottle caps and go to a field in Carolina. Then he would find some neighborhood boys and ask them to pitch him the bottle caps while he worked on his swing. For hours, Roberto would stand at the plate hitting the tiny bottle caps. When he was finished, he bent over and picked up all the caps for exercise.

"When I'm done hitting those bottle caps," he said, "a real baseball looks as big as a coconut!"

During the 1964 season, the baseball must have looked as big as the Goodyear blimp to Roberto. He pounded out 211 hits and won his second batting title with a .339 average. He hit 40 doubles, and he drove in 87 runs and scored 95. He was more patient at the plate, and his total of 51 walks was the highest of his career. He was the starting right fielder on the All-Star team and won his fourth straight Gold Glove Award.

For Roberto, it was a great individual season. But even though he was proud of his own accomplishments, he was frustrated. Ever since winning the World Championship in 1960, the Pirates had been struggling. In 1963 they finished eighth. They were only saved from last place because the National League had expanded to ten teams the year before. In 1964, the Pirates finished in a tie for sixth.

On August 18, 1964, Roberto celebrated his thirtieth birthday. It was a time for thinking about the past and looking toward the future. He was no longer the young boy who had left Barrio San Antón for the mysterious world of the major leagues. He was a mature and experienced player, a star. He had won one batting title and he was on his way to another. At home, he had a beautiful girl waiting for their wedding day. Life was good. But still, something was missing.

The next day, he met with a reporter at the Commodore Hotel in New York. "What goals do you have for the season?" the reporter asked.

Roberto sipped his iced tea as he considered

the question. "I have no goals," he said. "Have a good season. That is enough. Hitting for average is not the whole thing. My best year was 1960. The year 1961 was good, and so is 1964, but we did not win in 1961, and we are not winning this year. So it is not as good. Winning is fun."

Thousands of people filled the plaza in Carolina on November 14, 1964. It was a beautiful, sunny day, but they were not there for the sunshine. Inside the church of San Fernando, Roberto Clemente was marrying Vera Zabala. As the bride and groom walked down the old stone steps after the ceremony, the people in the plaza tried to get a glimpse of the happy couple. In Puerto Rico, Roberto was a great hero. He was a king, and the people of his native land were overjoyed that he had found his queen.

Roberto and Vera moved into a house that Roberto owned on three acres of land outside of Carolina. It was a very busy time. Roberto managed and played with the San Juan Senators in the winter league. He worked to set up baseball clinics for the youth of Puerto Rico and visited sick children in local hospitals. In his spare time, he did repairs around the house. Although he could afford to pay someone else to do the work, Roberto preferred to do it himself. He liked to keep his hands busy.

One day, Roberto was mowing the lawn. Suddenly, a rock got caught in the blades and shot out into his right leg. Roberto collapsed in pain. For the next few weeks, he stopped playing in the winter league, trying to give his leg time to heal. But in January, the fans and other players convinced him to give it a try during the annual Puerto Rican All-Star game. "Without Roberto Clemente," they asked, "how can it be an All-Star game?"

Although he could barely walk, Roberto stepped up to the plate as a pinch hitter. The injury had not affected his swing, and he smashed a hard line drive to right field. But as he limped to first base, his leg collapsed beneath him. He was rushed to the hospital, and a few days later, the doctors cut open his leg to drain a pool of blood in his thigh. "The operation was a complete success," they said. "Roberto will be ready to play by spring training."

The Pirate training camp opened on March 1, but Roberto Clemente was not there. The Pirates angrily announced that Roberto would be fined $100 for every day he was late. But they forgot about the fines when they discovered the reason for his absence. Roberto was lying in a Puerto Rican hospital with a fever of 105 degrees. His leg had healed, but his new illness was even more serious.

The doctors were not sure what was wrong. Perhaps it was malaria that he had caught on a trip to the Dominican Republic. Perhaps it was a typhoid infection from the pigs he raised on his land. Perhaps it was both. Whatever it was, Roberto was very sick. No one said he was "jaking it."

"Roberto, I don't think you should play this year." Roberto looked at his physician, Dr. Busó. He had lost 25 pounds during his illness, and though he had gained some of the weight back, he was still dangerously underweight. He felt tired and weak.

Vera agreed with Dr. Busó. "Why don't you retire for a year, then come back?" she asked.

"No," said Roberto. "I'll go and try it."

Vera stared at her husband. He was not the same strong man she had married just a few months earlier. How could he play a long, hard major-league season? "You can't play like this," she said. "You'll kill yourself."

Roberto was silent for a while. It was tempting to take the year off, to rest and come back stronger than ever. But then he thought of the games he would miss. It is hard to play when your body is weak, but it is worse not to play at all. "I like baseball," he said. "I love baseball and I know I have to play. It is my life."

Roberto was not the only Pirate who had problems with his health. After the 1964 season, Danny Murtaugh discovered that he had heart disease. Murtaugh stepped down as manager and took a less strenuous job in the Pirate organization. He was replaced by Harry Walker.

For Roberto, it was definitely a change for the better. Although he respected Murtaugh's ability as a manager, he did not like him as a person. He felt that Murtaugh never believed him when he was hurt and never gave him full credit for his contributions to the team. "Nobody had better years under Murtaugh than me," Roberto said, "but he acted like he didn't appreciate me. Instead of being friendly, he needled me."

Harry Walker took the opposite approach. He was a man who liked to be friends with everybody, and he definitely wanted to be friends with his star player. He was also a man who liked to talk, and what he liked to talk about was hitting. Unlike most managers, he knew the subject from personal experience. In 1947, Walker had led the National League with a .361 average.

Many of the Pirate players quickly grew tired of Walker's long lectures on the various methods of striking a ball with a bat, but Roberto was happy to listen. "Hey, I like to talk about baseball, too," he said.

In the spring of 1965, however, it looked like Roberto needed a doctor more than a hitting coach. He was twenty pounds underweight and still very weak from his illness. By the middle of May, he had no home runs and only nine runs batted in. His average was a weak .257. The Pirates were even worse, losing 24 out of their first 33 games.

During one series in St. Louis, Walker decided to give Roberto a rest on the bench. For years people had said that Roberto would not play hurt, that he was a crybaby and a jaker. The truth is that Roberto hated to sit in the dugout and watch out while other men played the game. It was even harder when Jerry Lynch, the man who replaced him in right field, got seven hits in ten at-bats.

Suddenly, the good relationship between Roberto and Harry Walker exploded. In a radio interview with St. Louis announcer Harry Caray, Walker said, "Superstars like Stan Musial and Ted Williams played with injuries." By the time this remark reached Roberto's ears it came out sounding like this: "Harry Walker says there's no reason you can't play."

Roberto was furious. After all, it was Walker himself who told him to take a rest. "I want to be traded," he said. "I cannot play for this man." Even during the difficult years under Danny Murtaugh, Roberto had never requested a trade.

Fortunately, Harry Walker knew how to calm down an angry superstar. He and Roberto met for breakfast and talked things over. Afterwards, they both agreed it was nothing but a big misunderstanding. "We tried to start him too soon after the malaria, and then rest him," Walker said. "It was the wrong way to do it."

The next day, Walker put Roberto into the game as a pinch hitter in the ninth inning. The Pirates were one run down with a man on third. Roberto hit a sacrifice fly to drive in the tying run. A few moments later, Manny Mota won the game with a single. Roberto was so happy, he practically carried Mota into the dugout.

Clemente was back and so were the Pirates. Roberto hit safely in 33 out of 34 games, raising his average all the way up to .340. The Pirates won 20 out of 22 games and climbed out of last place into the first division. By the end of the season, the Pirates were a solid third, only seven games behind the San Francisco Giants.

Roberto dropped off slightly to finish at .329. It was not his finest year, but it was the highest batting average in the major leagues. After surgery on his leg, after malaria or typhoid or both, Roberto Clemente had come back to win his third National League batting title.

Only four men in the modern history of the National League had ever won the batting title three or more times. Their names read like a list of greatness: Honus Wagner, Rogers Hornsby, Paul Waner, Stan Musial. Now there was a fifth name on the list: Roberto Clemente.

1 2

MVP

Every king needs a castle. Before the 1965 season, Roberto the batting king and Vera moved into a beautiful new home in Río Piedras, a suburb outside of San Juan. The house was set high on a hill with a breathtaking view of the city and San Juan Bay. The living room was 48 feet long with a huge sofa, thick carpeting, and a big picture window. There was a formal dining room and an open-air garden with tropical plants and a lily pond. Downstairs, next to the garage was a room for a billiards table and Roberto's trophies. There was even a small bridge that arched across a gully from the road to the front door.

On August 17, 1965, while Roberto Sr. was chasing his third batting title, Vera gave birth to Roberto Jr. It was the day before his father's 31st birthday. "If I'd waited a couple of hours," Vera said, "he would have been a birthday present." Roberto had sent Vera home to Puerto Rico to have the baby. "You were born there and I was born there," he said. "I want our child to be born there, too."

In Puerto Rico, Roberto had everything a man could want: a beautiful and loving wife, a luxurious home, and a fine son. His beloved parents lived a few miles away, and he was proud that he could help them in their old age. He was loved and respected by his countrymen. To the people of Puerto Rico, Roberto Clemente was more than a great baseball player. He was a living symbol of the island itself.

The United States was a different story. Since 1960, Roberto had hit .314, .351, .312, .320, .339, and .329. He had won three National League batting titles, and in two of those years, he had the highest average in the major leagues. In right field, he had won five straight Gold Glove Awards. He had played in the All-Star game every year and had led the Pittsburgh Pirates from last place to the World Championship.

To the people of Pittsburgh, he was as popular as he was in his homeland. But to the rest of the country, he was still the "Puerto Rican hot dog." "Sure, Clemente is a great hitter," they would say, "but he doesn't come through in the clutch." "He won't play hurt." "He doesn't hit for power." "He's not a team player."

There were many reasons for this attitude. Part of the problem was Roberto himself. He was a proud, sensitive man who said exactly what was on his mind. "If I am sick," he said, "I do not deny it." When people did not believe him, he became very angry. "We Latins get more excited than Americans," he admitted. "We have a lot of pepper blood. Sometimes I don't think Americans understand this."

Part of the problem was with the sportswriters and the other players. They would look at Roberto with his strong, muscular body and his handsome, healthy face, and they would refuse to believe that there was anything wrong with his back or his elbow or his stomach. When they saw him come to the plate and smash line drives like bullets off his bat, they would laugh among themselves. "I wish I felt so sick," they would say.

And part of the problem was Forbes Field. The first time that Roberto laid eyes on the distant left field wall, he knew that he would have to change his batting style. But if the fences were too long for home runs, they allowed plenty of room for hard line drives. Roberto learned to slash the ball around the park for singles, doubles, and triples.

In baseball, the line-drive hitter usually wins

the batting title, but it is the power hitter that gets the glory. In 1966, Roberto went for the glory.

"Bob, I want you to get 25 home runs and drive in 115. We'll need that to win the pennant."

Roberto looked at his manager, Harry Walker. They were sitting in Walker's office at the Pirate spring training camp in Fort Meyers, Florida. Under Danny Murtaugh, Roberto might have argued at such a suggestion. After all, he had won three batting titles by concentrating on hitting line drives. But he liked and respected Walker, and he was willing to do whatever the manager felt was necessary for the good of the team.

"Fine," Roberto said. "I'll just make a little adjustment with my hands."

"You're our leader now," Walker continued. "You need to set an example for the other players. If they see you hustle, they'll hustle, too."

"I always hustle," said Roberto seriously.

Walker smiled. "Of course you do, Bob. You go out and knock yourself out every day. I wish I had a dozen like you. But being a leader is more than just being a great player. I think you know what I'm talking about."

Roberto nodded his head. "Sure," he said, "I understand."

———————

"Hit the ball to me! C'mon, hit it to me! Don't try to pull it! Hit the ball to me!"

Roberto stood at third base on the Pirates' practice field. At the plate was Matty Alou, a young player from the Dominican Republic who had recently joined the Pirates in a trade with the San Francisco Giants.

Alou was a left-handed hitter, with a smooth, solid swing. Although he was a small man, he had tried to take advantage of the strong wind in San Francisco to pull the ball out of the park in right field. The approach was not very successful. In six years, Alou had only hit fourteen home runs in San Francisco. Harry Walker knew that Alou would have even less success in Forbes Field. He tried to convince him to change his style, but he was having trouble getting through to him. He turned the project over to Roberto.

"C'mon, punch the ball. Hit it at me. Don't try to pull it! Hit it to left! Hit it to left!"

Day after day, Roberto worked with Alou in spring training. During the regular season, the hard work paid off. Matty Alou raised his batting average 111 points and finished the year as the National League batting champion with an average of .342. For two years, Roberto had been the batting king. Now his pupil had inherited the crown.

While Alou took over the role of the singles hitter, Roberto began to hit the long ball. He started slowly. In mid-May, he was hitting only .285 with three home runs. Harry Walker gave him a few days rest and suddenly his bat caught fire. During one 11-game home stand in June, he hit .444 with 28 hits and 6 home runs. Two of the homers were long blasts over an iron gate in right-center field that was 436 feet from the plate.

Led by Roberto, the Pirates were locked in a tight pennant race with the Dodgers and the Giants. All summer long, the lead shifted back and forth. To relieve some of the pressure, Pirate catcher Jim Pagliaroni invented the "Black Maxes."

Pagliaroni and some other players had gone to see a film called *The Blue Max*, which was about a World War I flying ace. They liked it so much that they decided to start wearing old-fashioned flying helmets and goggles in the clubhouse. Relief pitcher ElRoy Face walked around with a real pirate's hat, complete with skull and crossbones. Some teams get tense when the pennant race goes down to the wire, but the Pirates just got looser and looser. "We haven't got a sane guy on the ball club," said Pagliaroni.

When the games got tough, the Pirates used the

power of the Green Weenie. In 1960, Pirate trainer Danny Whelan found a giant green plastic hot dog. He noticed that whenever he pointed it at an opposing pitcher, the Pirates started hitting. When he pointed it at a Pirate pitcher, it magically produced strike-outs. In 1966, the Green Weenie was mass-produced. Thousands of Pirate fans sat in Forbes Field with green plastic hot dogs ready to come to the aid of the Bucs.

Roberto never joined the Black Maxes or carried a Green Weenie, but he joked and laughed with the rest of the team. On the playing field, he just kept hitting. In early September, the Pirates played the Cubs at Forbes Field. It was the fifth inning and the Bucs were holding on to a slim 1–0 lead. There were two men on as Roberto came to the plate.

The Cub pitcher was Ferguson Jenkins, a tall, powerful right-hander. Jenkins leaned back and fired a pitch over the outside corner. Roberto reached out and smashed it into the right-field seats. The Pirates were ahead, 4–0.

As Roberto trotted around the bases, the fans jumped to their feet and showered him with applause. It was a big hit in the middle of a pennant race. But it was more than that. For Roberto, it was the 2,000th hit of his major-league career. In 1966, only eight other active players had 2,000 hits. It was Roberto's 23rd home run of the season, which tied his own personal record. And it was his 101st RBI, the first time he had ever driven in more than 100 runs.

Harry Walker had said the Pirates needed Roberto to hit for power in order to win the pennant. Roberto held up his end of the bargain, but the Pirates faded in the last two weeks of the season, finally finishing in third place. The Dodgers won the pennant behind the brilliant pitching of Sandy Koufax. They may also have had some help from the Mexican Sombrero, a giant hat that they used to combat the power of the Green Weenie.

For the Pirates, it was an exciting but disappointing year. For Roberto Clemente, it was the finest season of his career. He hit 29 home runs and had 119 RBI. He scored 105 runs and had 31 doubles and 11 triples. Despite changing his batting style to hit for more power, he finished fifth in the league with an average of .317. In the field he won his sixth consecutive Gold Glove Award and led the league by throwing out 17 base runners. But even more important than his personal statistics, he had been willing to sacrifice his own average for the good of the team. He was a leader.

"There's no question about it," said Harry Walker,

"Clemente has been the guts of this club. If he's not the league's most valuable player, I'm nuts."

Roberto was working on his farm outside Carolina when the results of the MVP voting were announced. The race was close. Sandy Koufax had a great year with 27 wins, 27 complete games, an earned-run average of 1.73, and a league-leading 317 strike-outs. The Dodgers had won the pennant while the Pirates had finished third. But when the votes were counted, Roberto Clemente was named the Most Valuable Player in the National League.

Roberto was very happy. After twelve years in the major leagues, the sportswriters had finally given him the respect he felt he deserved. But just as he had felt when he won his first batting title in 1961, Roberto was proudest of the fact that he could share his honor with the people of Puerto Rico.

"When I was a kid," he said, "I felt that baseball was great for America. Always, they said Babe Ruth was the best there ever was. They said you'd really have to be something to be like Babe Ruth. But Babe Ruth was an American player. What we needed was a Puerto Rican player they could say that about, someone to look up to and try to equal.

"I've won the batting title three times and now I've won the MVP. This makes me happy because now the people feel that if I could do it, then they could do it. The kids have someone to look to and to follow. That's why I like to work with kids so much. I show them what baseball has done for me and maybe they will work harder and try harder and be better men."

I'm Lucky to Be Alive

Roberto lay flat on the table as Pirate trainer Tony Bartirome massaged the aching muscles in his neck. This was his favorite time of the day. It was a half hour before the game, and Roberto closed his eyes, imagining every pitch of the upcoming contest.

In his mind, he could see himself at the plate, digging into the farthest corner of the batter's box. He could see the first pitch, a fastball inside for ball one. He could see the next pitch, a slider on the outside corner. He could see himself reach out and smash a hard line drive to right field.

Suddenly a mysterious voice emerged from beneath the trainer's table. "Good morning, Mr. Clemente, this is your neck. Your assignment today will be to go three-for-four with a bases-loaded double, and throw out two runners at first base. In five seconds, this tape will self-destruct. Phsssssst!"

Roberto opened his eyes and looked around the

Pirate clubhouse as if he were trying to figure out where the voice was coming from. Of course, he knew it was Steve Blass underneath the table. Blass was a young Pirate pitcher who had joined the club the year before. Roberto called him *loquito*, which means "little crazy one."

When the joke was over, Roberto closed his eyes again and went back to thinking about the game. Inning by inning, he watched every pitch in his mind. By the time he actually took the field he would be ready for anything.

After winning the MVP award, Roberto signed a new contract with the Pirates for $100,000 a year. He was now one of only five players in baseball who made $100,000 or more. The others were Willie Mays, Hank Aaron, Mickey Mantle, and Frank Robinson.

Roberto wanted to show the Pirates and their fans that he was worth every penny. In 1967, he won his fourth batting title with an average of .357. It was the highest average of his career. He had 209 hits, 23 home runs, and 110 RBI. By now, the Gold Glove Award had become automatic for him. Once again he led the outfielders of the league by gunning down 17 base runners with his strong right arm.

The Pirates did not do as well. After two strong seasons in third place, they dropped to sixth. In July, Harry Walker was fired as manager and Danny Murtaugh returned to his old job for the rest of the season. Roberto was not happy about the change, but he had a new and more mature attitude. "I can play for any manager," he said.

Murtaugh was a little older and wiser, too. "I can always get along with a man who hits .350," he said with a smile.

In 1968, Murtaugh went back into retirement, and Larry Shepard took over as manager of the Pirates. Shepard almost lost his star player before the season began.

Roberto was at home in Río Piedras, doing some repair work on a patio. The patio was on two levels, and he was climbing a set of iron bars to reach the second level. Suddenly, the heavy bar broke away from the wall, and Roberto fell to the ground below. He landed painfully on the back of his neck and rolled over on his right shoulder. He rolled and rolled down the hillside until he was finally stopped by a low wall. Beyond the wall was a steep cliff.

"I'm lucky to be alive," Roberto said. "I could have been killed in that fall." As it was, he suffered a torn muscle in his right shoulder. The injury made it difficult to swing the bat with power and, by the middle of the season, he was only hitting .245. For the first time in nine years, he was not chosen to the National League All-Star team.

In the second half of the season, he managed to raise his average to .291. For most players, that would be a very respectable average, but for Roberto it was the first time since 1959 that he had failed to hit over .300.

After the season, Roberto began to think of retiring. "Any time you're not doing your best," he said, "you are stealing the fans' money. And I don't call myself a thief."

At home in Río Piedras, Roberto talked to Vera about his feelings. Vera understood her husband's frustration. It would be nice to have him at home. There were two Clemente sons now, and a third was on the way. But she knew that he loved baseball almost as much as he loved her and their children.

"Never quit when you're down," she said. "You have to give it another try. If you want to quit after another year, I won't say a word."

By the time Roberto reported to the Pirate training camp that spring, his right shoulder had improved and he looked forward to a good season. But then, while he was chasing a long fly ball, he smashed into the right-field fence and injured his left shoulder. "Now my bad shoulder is good, but my good shoulder is bad," he said.

The shoulder injury continued to bother him as the Pirates began the regular season. In early April, he smashed into the wall at Forbes Field while chasing a foul ball. Now he had a pulled muscle in his left leg to go along with the shoulder problem. A few days later, the Pirates were playing the Phillies, and Roberto had one of the worst games of his career.

In the first inning, he struck out. In his next two at bats, he hit into double plays. In the top of the eighth inning, he let a ball go through his legs in right field, allowing the Phillies to score a run. As he came to the plate in the bottom of the eighth, a strange sound emerged from the stands. At first it sounded like the buzzing of a thousand bumblebees. Then slowly, it grew louder and clearer. "Boooooo! Boooooo!" The fans at Forbes Field were booing Roberto Clemente!

At the plate, Roberto took off his batting helmet and waved it toward the stands. Suddenly, half the boos turned into applause. Later, in the Pirate clubhouse, Roberto said, "I was not trying to be smart when I waved my helmet. I was just trying to tell them that they could do whatever they want. The fans of Pittsburgh have cheered me a lot during the years. There's always a first time for the booing."

Roberto continued to struggle through the early part of the season. In May, after a frustrating game in San Diego, he called Vera long distance. She was home in Puerto Rico, waiting for the birth of their third child. "I want to quit," he said. "Finish the road trip," Vera replied. "Then if you come back to Pittsburgh and you don't feel any better, it will be all right to quit. That's a promise, OK?"

"OK, you're the boss," said Roberto. "But if I don't feel better when I get back to Pittsburgh, then it is all over."

After hanging up the phone, Roberto went down to the lobby of the hotel and ran into his fellow Pirate outfielder, Willie Stargell. Stargell had a bag of fried chicken in his hand. "There's a place you can get some just down the road," he told Roberto.

Stargell was the Pirate expert on fried chicken, so Roberto walked down the road to get a bag of his own. On the way back to the hotel, a car pulled up alongside him. There were four men inside. One of them pointed a gun at Roberto. "Get in," he said. Roberto got in the car, still holding his hot bag of fried chicken. The men drove him away from the lights of the city and into the dark, deserted hills.

They shoved him out of the car and ordered him to take off his clothes. Then they took his wallet, which held $250 in cash, and the All-Star ring he had worn ever since his great performance in 1961.

Roberto was sure the men were going to kill him. "They already had the pistol in my mouth," he said later. As he stood in the dark hills, he thought of his wife and children at home in Puerto Rico. He would never see them again. He would never play another baseball game.

One of the men spoke Spanish, and Roberto began to plead with him in his native language. "I am a ballplayer," he said. "You can look in my wallet. There is a membership card in the Baseball Players' Association. If you really need the money, take it, but don't kill me. Don't kill anybody for money."

When the men discovered who he was, they gave him back his clothes. "Don't forget to put your tie on," one of them said. "We want you to look good." They returned his wallet and his ring and dropped him off a few blocks from his hotel. As the car sped away, Roberto let out a long, deep breath. He was safe.

Suddenly, the car backed up. Roberto searched the ground for a rock to throw. They've changed their mind, he thought. They're going to kill me after all. One of the men rolled down the window and held out a small brown bag. "Here," he said. Roberto took the bag and stared in amazement as the car drove away again. Then he looked down at the bag in his hand. It was the fried chicken.

For a moment, Roberto stood in the middle of the road, thinking about the strange events of the night. Then he turned and walked back to his hotel, still carrying the brown paper bag. The chicken was cold now, but it didn't matter. He was suddenly very hungry. It felt good to be alive.

After his brush with death, Roberto began to hit with his old enthusiasm. In the next month, he raised his average from .226 to .314. By the end of the year, he was batting .345, second only to Pete Rose at .348. It was a spectacular comeback after his off year in 1968. But even while he concentrated on his own performance at the plate, Roberto continued to be a leader in the Pirate clubhouse.

When the team faded in the middle of the season, manager Larry Shepard placed the blame on a rookie catcher named Manny Sanguillen. Sanguillen was a powerfully built, good-natured player from Panama. When he first joined the Pirates, he had a smile for everyone, but his easy smile began to fade in the high-pressure spotlight of the major leagues.

As Roberto saw the young Latin player struggling to be accepted, he remembered his own early years in the league. In 1955, there was no one to stand up for Roberto. In 1969, he stood up for Sanguillen.

In one game, Sanguillen was picked off twice at first base. Afterwards, Roberto went into the club house and stuck a broomstick through a big piece of cardboard. When Sanguillen walked in with a miserable look on his face, Roberto stood grinning ear to ear as he mysteriously moved the broomstick around like the control on an airplane.

"It is a new machine," he said. "I have just bought it. I am going to use it to take control of your body whenever you get on base."

1 4

I Don't Have the Words

On June 28, 1970, the Pittsburgh Pirates played their last game at Forbes Field. For Roberto, it was an emotional moment. "I spent half my life there," he said. Two and a half weeks later, after a long road trip, the team moved into their new home at Three Rivers Stadium.

Built at the junction of the Ohio, Allegheny, and Monongahela rivers, the new park was an ultra-modern stadium with an evenly shaped field and artificial turf. After sixteen years of playing on grass, Roberto quickly adapted to the new surface. On a ball hit into the gap between right and center field, he'd slide on the carpet, pick up the ball, and spring to his feet to make the throw all in one graceful motion.

The Pirates seemed to like their new home as well. The year before, the National League had been divided into two divisions. In their first two weeks at Three Rivers, the Pirates passed the New York Mets and took over first place in the National League East.

On July 24, the Pirates were scheduled to play the Houston Astros. Before the game, Roberto stood on the new green carpet and looked around the stadium. There were over 43,000 fans. In the right-field stands, he could see hundreds of *pavas*, the big white straw hats worn by Puerto Rican workers in the sugar fields. The people of Puerto Rico had come to join the people of Pittsburgh in his honor. It was Roberto Clemente Night.

On the field with Roberto were Vera and their three children, Roberto Jr., Luis, and tiny Enrique. Doña Luisa and Don Melchor sat beside them. Don Melchor was ninety years old now. He was thin and frail, but his eyes were still strong and clear. The trip to Pittsburgh was his first time on an airplane.

Heriberto Nieves, the mayor of Carolina, also sat on the field in honor of his city's most famous son. There were other officials from Puerto Rico and many important citizens of Pittsburgh. The entire program was broadcast by satellite to Puerto Rico.

As the ceremony began, the other Latin players on the Pirates walked up to Roberto in single file.

Each placed a hand on his shoulder and bent forward in an *abrazo*, an embrace. A young Puerto Rican businessman named Juan Jiménez presented Roberto with a scroll containing 300,000 signatures from the people of Puerto Rico. Out of a population of around 3,000,000, one out of every ten Puerto Ricans had signed the scroll.

Roberto was presented with many other gifts and trophies, including a brand-new car. At Roberto's request, thousands of dollars were donated to help the crippled children at Pittsburgh's Children's Hospital. Finally, it came time for Roberto to speak. The announcer, Ramiro Martínez, asked him to say a few words in Spanish to the people who were watching and listening in Puerto Rico.

"Before anything," Roberto began, "I want to send an *abrazo* to my brothers . . ." Suddenly he turned away from the microphone. His eyes were wet with tears. Martínez whispered some words of encouragement. After a few moments, Roberto continued.

"I want to dedicate this triumph to all the mothers in Puerto Rico. I haven't the words to express my gratitude. I only ask that those who are watching this program be close to their parents, ask for their blessing and embrace . . . and those friends who are watching or listening, shake hands in the friendship that unites all Puerto Ricans."

When he was finished, Roberto looked over at his mother and his father. There were tears in their eyes and tears in his eyes, too. There, in front of 43,000 people and tens of thousands more watching on television, Roberto did not have to say another word to show the love and respect he felt for Don Melchor and Doña Luisa.

Now it was time for the game. Before the "Star-Spangled Banner," the fans and players stood for "La Borinqueña," the national anthem of Puerto Rico. As the Astros came up to bat in the first inning, the Puerto Rican fans in right field serenaded Roberto with a special song written just for that night. "Roberto Clemente, orgulla de Puerto Rico," it began. "Roberto Clemente, the pride of Puerto Rico."

Behind the great pitching of Dock Ellis, the Pirates routed the Astros 11–0. Roberto had two hits and made a fantastic sliding catch in right field. Late in the game, with the Pirates already on their way to an easy win, Roberto made another diving catch of a foul ball. As he stood to his feet, there was blood seeping through the knee of his uniform pants. Later, when reporters asked him why he risked hurting himself on a play that didn't really matter, he shrugged and said, "It's the only way I know how to play baseball."

With two out in the top of the ninth inning, Manager Danny Murtaugh removed Roberto from the game. Murtaugh had returned at the beginning of the season for his third turn as the Pirate manager. This time there were no conflicts between the tough manager and his fiery superstar. As Roberto trotted in from right field, the fans showed their appreciation with a standing ovation. In the Pirate dugout, Murtaugh stood and applauded with them.

After the game, a reporter asked Roberto about his tears during the ceremony. "In a moment like this," he said, "you can see a lot of years in a few minutes. You can see everything firm and you can see everything clear. I don't know if I cried, but I am not ashamed to cry. I would say a man never cries from pain or disappointment. But if you know the history of our island, you ought to remember we're a sentimental people. I don't have the words to say how I feel when I step on that field and know that so many are behind me, and know that so many represent my island and Latin America."

Roberto had a number of injuries during the 1970 season. But when Danny Murtaugh tried to rest him on the bench, he kept on playing. "I wanted to rest him," Murtaugh said, "but he insisted on playing because we haven't been winning. He's doing everything he can to get us rolling."

Years before, it was Murtaugh who demanded that Roberto play with injuries. Now it was Roberto who refused to rest. Times had changed.

In late August, the Pirates were playing the Dodgers in Los Angeles. During a long 16-inning game, Roberto had five hits in seven at-bats. He drove in one run and scored another as the Bucs finally edged the Dodgers 2–1. The next night, the Pirates had an easier time, beating the Dodgers 11–0. Again Roberto had five hits, including a double and a home run. It was the first time in modern baseball history that a player had ten hits in two consecutive games.

After his record-breaking performance, Roberto led the National League with an average of .363. But in early September, he reinjured his back while swinging too hard at a pitch. By the end of the season, his average had dropped slightly to .352. The Pirates, with Danny Murtaugh back in charge, won the National League East but lost to the Cincinnati Reds in the divisional playoffs. The World Series would have to wait.

After the season, Roberto was asked if he still

wanted to retire. He was 36 years old now, and many players his age had given up the game long ago. "Let's see," he said with a smile. "I hit .345 last year and .352 this year. No, I don't think I want to quit now."

Roberto looked at the men who had come to see him at his home in Río Piedras. It was January of 1971, and he was busy managing the San Juan Senators in the winter league. Even though he had five of his Pirate teammates playing for him in Puerto Rico, the team was struggling. But that was a different problem. Now there was something else on his mind.

"Roberto," said one of the men, "we are here to ask you a great favor. You are a respected citizen and a fine man. Time and time again, you have proven your love for the people of Puerto Rico. We need a man with your intelligence and leadership. We want you to run for mayor of Carolina."

Roberto listened respectfully to the man's words. He considered the offer. Certainly he was popular enough in Carolina to win the election. As mayor he could do many things to help his people. But the more he thought about it, the more he was sure that he did not have the personality for politics. He would have to help in other ways.

"There's no use for me to say yes," he said. "Say

I was elected and a situation came up where I have to compromise. I cannot compromise."

That winter, Roberto had other concerns as well. Don Melchor fell seriously ill and had to have surgery. Before the operation, Roberto sat at his father's bedside, looking down at his worn and tired face. It is only on the outside that he is old, Roberto thought. On the inside, his heart is young.

Don Melchor looked weakly up at his son. Over the years, he had learned much more about baseball. He knew that the Pirates had come very close in 1970. And he knew that Roberto wanted to play in one more World Series before he retired. "Momen," he said, "you can make it better this year."

Roberto smiled. He appreciated Don Melchor's encouragement, but his father's health was more important to him than the World Series. "No, Papá," he said, "you go and make it better this year."

15

Now Everyone Knows

In the Pirate locker room, Dock Ellis danced and shouted to the loud music booming out of the stereo. "Funky! Funky! Yeah!" It was August of 1971, and Ellis was feeling good. The Pirates were on top of the National League East by eleven games, and Ellis, their star pitcher, had won thirteen games in a row. Suddenly, Pirate trainer Tony Bartirome turned down the music.

"Whose idea was that?" asked Ellis.

Bartirome pointed to Roberto, who was lying on the trainer's table having a rubdown after the game.

Ellis broke into a big grin. "Did you notice how the room went silent?" he asked. Then he started imitating Roberto—limping across the floor, holding his back and neck, and speaking in a Spanish accent. "Oh, I not like I used to be. I a leettle bit of an old man now."

Manny Sanguillen jumped up and got into the

act. "Did you see Clemente slide last night?" he screamed as he slid across the floor. "I want to go help him up, the old man!" Roberto continued to lie on the trainer's table, naked except for a white towel. He pretended not to notice the younger Pirates' teasing. But inside he was laughing with them. In his seventeenth major-league season, he was having more fun than he'd ever had before.

For years, the Pirates had been a solid hitting team, but in 1971 they were awesome. They took the lead in April and never gave it up. Roberto had another fine year, batting .341 with 86 RBI. Willie Stargell led the National League with 48 home runs and 125 RBI. Manny Sanguillen hit .323, and the other young Pirate batters delivered key hits throughout the season.

In early October, the Pirates played the San Francisco Giants for the right to represent the National League in the World Series. After losing the first game 5–4, the Pirates came back to win the series three games to one. In the final game, Roberto had three RBI, including a hard single up the middle to drive in the winning run.

Afterwards, Roberto sat quietly on Tony Bartirome's training table while the other players sprayed each other with champagne and beer. A circle of reporters stood around him. "I am happy," he said, "very happy, but I don't have to jump up and down. Some people think I am strange because I don't jump up and down."

John Galbreath, the owner of the Pirates, worked his way through the reporters to shake Roberto's hand. "You're everything we think you are," he said. "You never let us down. You come through every time—you're the greatest."

"Do you really think you're the greatest?" asked a reporter.

Roberto thought for a moment. For years, they had said that Willie Mays was the greatest. But Mays was a few years older than Roberto. He had not played very well in the playoffs.

"How do you measure a man?" Roberto said. "How can you compare one man with another unless you've seen them both? I cannot tell about other men who played long ago. I saw Mays. To me, Willie Mays is the greatest who ever played. But he is forty and he has had his days. He is tired."

One of the Pirates walked up to Roberto and stood ready to spray him with beer. "No, no," Roberto cried, "I got a bad eye." With the rest of the team laughing in delight, big Bob Veale, a 6′ 6″ pitcher, picked Roberto up in his arms and carried him into the shower. "As you can see," Roberto said to the reporters, "there are no privileges on the Pirates."

In 1960, the Yankees were expected to sweep the Pirates in the World Series. In 1971, it was the Baltimore Orioles. Under manager Earl Weaver, the Orioles had led the American League East for three straight years. In 1970, they defeated the Cincinnati Reds four games to one in the World Series. Although they did not have as many great hitters as the Pirates, they had four twenty-game winners on their pitching staff. They finished the regular season with eleven straight victories and rolled over the Oakland A's in the playoffs in three straight games.

The first two games of the World Series were played in Baltimore's Memorial Stadium. Behind the pitching of Dave McNally and Jim Palmer, the Orioles kept on rolling, defeating the Pirates by scores of 5–3 and 11–3. After the second game, the Pirates were frustrated and depressed. Since 1903, only five teams had come back to win the World Series after losing the first two games. "Now our backs are to the wall," said Danny Murtaugh.

Roberto tried to cheer them up. He had a single and a double in each of the first two games, and he didn't plan to stop now. "Don't worry," he said.

"I'll get you up when we get to Pittsburgh. I will hit those Baltimore pitchers like we're taking batting practice."

In the third game, the Pirates sent Steve Blass to the mound. On the surface, Roberto Clemente and Steve Blass were as different as night and day. Roberto was a quiet, dignified black man from the sugar fields of Puerto Rico. Blass was a nervous, "flaky" white man from a small town in Connecticut. But together, Clemente and Blass put the Pirates back in the Series.

In the first inning, Roberto drove in the first Pirate run with an infield ground ball. The Pirates added a run in the sixth, but the Orioles came back with a run of their own in the top of the seventh. The score was 2–1 as Roberto stepped to the plate in the bottom of the seventh. Steve Blass was pitching a brilliant game for the Pirates, but Mike Cuellar was equally brilliant for the Orioles.

Roberto arched his back and rolled his neck around. As he took his practice swings, he stared out at Cuellar. Cuellar was a fine left-hander from Cuba. That winter, he had played under Roberto on the San Juan Senators. When Roberto asked him to become a relief pitcher, he quit the team in anger. Now the two men were meeting in a crucial moment of the World Series.

Cuellar leaned back and fired the pitch. Roberto swung hard, but instead of meeting the ball solidly, he topped an easy bouncer to Cuellar on the mound. It looked like a sure out, but Cuellar was so surprised to see Roberto racing at full speed down the line that he rushed his throw and pulled first baseman Boog Powell off the bag. As Roberto stood at first base, he thought back to the 1960 World Series. In the seventh game, he had beat out another easy grounder to turn the Series around for the Pirates. Maybe it would work again.

On the mound, Cuellar was frustrated by his throwing error. He walked Willie Stargell to put men on first and second. The next batter was Bob Robertson. Danny Murtaugh decided to play it safe and move the runners to second and third. He gave Robertson the bunt sign, but the big first baseman missed the sign and crushed the next pitch over the 385-foot mark in right-center field. The Pirate fans at Three Rivers Stadium jumped to their feet as Clemente, Stargell, and Robertson trotted around the bases.

With a 5–1 lead, Steve Blass coasted through the last two innings to give the Pirates their first Series victory. The next evening, the Pirates tied it at two apiece with a 4–3 victory. It was the first night game in World Series history, and over sixty million people watched on national television.

In the third inning, Roberto smashed a hard, high drive down the right-field line. On television, it looked like a home run, but the umpire called it a foul ball. While Danny Murtaugh argued angrily with the umpire, Roberto stood calmly in front of the Pirate dugout. When the argument was over, he stepped back up to the plate and smashed a single to right.

After the game, a New York sportswriter named Dick Young wrote: "The best ballplayer in the World Series, maybe in the whole world, is Roberto Clemente. . . . Maybe some guys hit it harder, and some throw it harder, and one or two run faster, although I doubt that, but nobody puts it all together like Roberto." Young was one of the most respected sportswriters in the country. After years of being ignored, Roberto was finally receiving the national attention he deserved.

In Game 5, the Pirates won 4–0 behind the three-hit pitching of Nelson Briles. As they flew back to Baltimore, the underdogs were up three games to two. But the Orioles came back to edge the Pirates by a score of 3–2, despite a triple and a home run by Roberto. Before the final game, Roberto sat in the clubhouse talking with Howie Haak. Back in 1954, Haak had been one of the Pirate scouts who recognized Roberto's talent with the Montreal Royals.

"Howie," Roberto said seriously, "you have been a good friend of mine, so I want you to be the first to know. If we win today's game, I am going to retire."

It was a cool, cloudy Sunday afternoon as the Baltimore Orioles took the field for the seventh game. The pitchers were the same as in Game 3: Mike Cuellar vs. Steve Blass. For the first three innings, they were both unhittable. When Roberto came to bat in the top of the fourth inning, Cuellar had retired the first eleven Pirate batters. Only two balls had even gotten out of the infield.

Roberto arched his back and rolled his neck. He stepped into the box and took his practice swings. Then he crouched into his batting stance and glared out at Cuellar. A few days earlier, a Baltimore reporter had written that Roberto did not have the power to pull the ball to left field. I will show them power, he thought. When Cuellar came inside with a high curveball, Roberto stepped back and pounded the ball over the left-field fence. The Pirates were ahead 1–0.

In the eighth inning, the Pirates added another run on a single by Willie Stargell and a double by

José Pagán, a veteran infielder from Puerto Rico. Through the first seven innings, Steve Blass had allowed only two hits. But in the bottom of the eighth, he ran into trouble and the Orioles scored to make the score 2–1 Pirates.

It was all they would get. In the ninth, Blass set the Orioles down on eight pitches as the Baltimore fans sat silently in their seats. After the final out, catcher Manny Sanguillen ran like a madman out to the mound. Blass leaped into his arms and screamed with joy. The Pittsburgh Pirates were Champions of the World!

As Roberto fought his way through the fans on the field and into the Pirate dugout, he saw Vera standing in the front row. There were tears running down her beautiful face, tears of joy. "Don't quit now," she said. "Baseball's your life." Roberto smiled and nodded. He had already changed his mind.

In the locker room, Roberto was surrounded by reporters from all over the country. In 1960, Roberto was an important part of the championship team, but other men had gotten more credit. In 1971, there was no question that Roberto Clemente was the Most Valuable Player of the World Series. He had batted .414 with twelve hits including two home runs, one triple, and two doubles. As in 1960, he had at least one hit in every game. He had fielded brilliantly and had held the Oriole base runners in check with his powerful arm.

"I want everyone to know that this is the way I play all the time," said Roberto. "All season, every season, I gave everything I have to this game. The press call me a crybaby, a hypochondriac . . . they say that I'm not a team player. Now everyone knows the way Roberto Clemente plays. They saw me in the World Series. Mentally, I will be a different person now."

After he had talked with the newspaper reporters, Roberto was asked to do a television interview. "Before I say anything," he began, "I want to say something in Spanish to my mother and father." Looking into the camera, Roberto spoke directly to Don Melchor and Doña Luisa, who were watching at home in Puerto Rico. "On this, the proudest day of my life," he said, "I ask your blessing."

The Pirates continued their celebration on the flight back to Pittsburgh. As Roberto and Vera walked down the aisle of the plane, Roberto noticed Steve Blass sitting with his wife, Karen. The two Pirate heroes had not really seen each other since the game. There had been interviews, flowing champagne, and a mad rush to get to the airport. "Where have you been?" Roberto asked. "Blass, let me embrace you."

16

The Least I Can Do

Before the 1971 season, Roberto received an award from the baseball writers of Houston. In front of 800 people, he gave a speech that one writer remembered as "the most inspirational talk we've ever had." It was a long way from the days when the sportswriters made fun of his English. He still had a strong Spanish accent, but his words were clear and from the heart.

"Accomplishment is something you can't buy," he said. "Any time you have the opportunity to accomplish something for somebody who comes behind you and you don't do it, you are wasting your time on this earth."

A year later, after his brilliant performance in the World Series, Roberto was a bigger hero than ever before. Not only in Puerto Rico and Pittsburgh, but in the rest of the United States, too. He spent the winter receiving many more awards in different parts of the country, including a new automobile given to the MVP of the Series. But he never thought these awards were just for himself. They were for all the other Latin and black players who had struggled to be accepted in the major leagues.

"My greatest satisfaction," he said, "comes from helping to erase the old opinion about Latin Americans and blacks. People never questioned our ability, but they considered us inferior to their station in life. Simply because many of us were poor, we were thought to be low-class."

For the first time in many years, Roberto did not play at all in the Puerto Rican winter league. He was 37 years old now, and he had to save his energy for the major-league season. But there was another reason as well. In between his many public appearances, he was working very hard on a new project.

For years, Roberto had dreamed of building a *Ciudad Deportiva*, a Sports City where the poor children of Puerto Rico could come and learn about sports from good coaches with real equipment. He had never forgotten the muddy field of Barrio San Antón where he and his friends played with a rag ball and a guava stick bat. He believed that the Sports City would help teach children the values they needed in the rest of their lives: to give their best effort, to work together as a team, and to respect the rules.

"It is the biggest ambition in my life," he said. "I want to have three baseball fields, a swimming pool, basketball, tennis, a lake where fathers and sons can get together, all kinds of recreational sports. . . . It will be open to everybody. No matter who they are. And after I open the first one in Puerto Rico, I will open others. I will do this thing because this is what God meant me to do. Baseball is just something that gave me the chance to do this."

Roberto looked out the window of the Pirates' chartered airplane. They were approaching the Pittsburgh airport, returning home after a long road trip. Suddenly another plane appeared out of nowhere and passed within fifty feet of the Pirates' plane. Roberto felt his heart skip a beat as he watched the near-collision.

In the seat beside him was Manny Sanguillen. The two men had become close friends over the last few years. On the surface they were very different—Manny with his easy, happy smile; Roberto with his serious, thoughtful look. But in their hearts, they shared a love for baseball and the people of Latin America.

"Sangy," Roberto said, "I've got to get those

3,000 hits this year. I might get sick or die, and no other Latin player will do it."

Manny put his arm around Roberto's shoulders and gave him a friendly squeeze. "Don't talk like that," he said with a grin. "You live good and you play good. The hits will come."

In almost one hundred years of major league baseball, only ten players had gotten 3,000 hits. At the beginning of the 1972 season, Roberto needed 118 hits to reach the 3,000 milestone. In a normal season, he would get that many by July or August. But in 1972, Roberto was bothered by many injuries and illnesses. It looked like number 3,000 would have to wait until 1973.

Going into the last 26 games of the season, Roberto was still 25 hits short of his goal. But then suddenly he began to pound the ball around the National League parks with the strength of a younger man. On September 28, he got hit number 2,999 against Steve Carlton in Philadelphia. Afterwards, he asked to be removed from the lineup. The Pirates were heading back to Pittsburgh after the game. Roberto wanted to get number 3,000 at home.

The next night, the Pirates were playing the New York Mets. It was a cold and rainy evening, but 24,000 fans came out to Three Rivers Stadium to watch Roberto take a swing at history. On the mound for the Mets was Tom Seaver, a brilliant pitcher with a red-hot fastball. In his first time at bat, Roberto chopped a little bouncer off of Seaver's glove. As Roberto tore down the first base line, the second baseman came in to field it, but the ball bounced off his glove, too. Roberto stood safe at first.

A big "H" appeared on the electronic scoreboard, and the crowd exploded in celebration. On the field, the umpire called time and the Mets first baseman presented Roberto with the ball. No one noticed that the big "H" had disappeared. Suddenly the scoreboard lit up with a new message: "E-4." The official scorer had ruled it an error on the second baseman.

Seaver held Roberto hitless the rest of the game. The next afternoon, the mood in the Pirate clubhouse was tense. Everybody was talking and thinking about the 3,000th hit. Everybody except Roberto—he pretended it didn't matter. Finally José Pagán turned to his fellow Puerto Rican and said, "Roberto, do me a favor. Lend me your bat, and I'll hit number 3,000 for you!"

The Met pitcher that afternoon was a young left-hander named Jon Matlack, who was on his way to being chosen National League Rookie of the Year. All season long, Matlack had held Roberto without a hit. In the first inning, Roberto struck out swinging. As he stepped up to the plate in the fourth, Willie Stargell handed him a bat and said, "Go get it." Roberto arched his back and rolled his neck around. He stepped into the batter's box, his right foot deep against the back line. He took his practice swings. Then he crouched, cocked his bat and waited for the pitch. Matlack leaned back and fired a fastball. Roberto watched it sail over the plate for strike one.

On the next pitch, Matlack came inside with a curveball. Roberto leaned back and smashed a hard line drive into the gap in left-center field. As the ball bounced on the artificial turf and rebounded off the outfield wall, Roberto raced around first and came into second standing up. There was no need to look at the scoreboard. It was a clean, hard-hit double.

As the Pittsburgh fans showered him with applause, Roberto stood at second and lifted his batting helmet. Once again the umpire called time and Roberto was presented with the historic ball. This time there was no second-guessing. This time it was for real.

After the game, Roberto said, "I dedicate that hit to the person I owe the most in professional baseball, Roberto Marín."

At home in Puerto Rico, Señor Marín listened

to Roberto's words on the radio. He closed his eyes and thought back to the day he first saw Roberto on the muddy field of Barrio San Antón. So many years had passed—almost a quarter of a century—but he could still picture young Roberto Clemente standing in the twilight. Señor Marín had never seen Roberto play in the United States. But now the boy he had discovered hitting tin cans with a stick was the eleventh man in history to have 3,000 major-league hits.

Roberto never got his hit number 3,001. The Pirates won the divisional title for the third year in a row, and Roberto sat out the last games of the regular season to rest up for the playoffs. In an exciting five-game series with the Cincinnati Reds, the Pirates lost in the final inning of the fifth game. Roberto had four hits in the series, including a home run, a double, and seven RBI. But hits in the play-offs and World Series are not counted in a player's career totals. For Roberto Clemente, 3,000 was the end.

On the morning of December 23, 1972, a powerful earthquake shook the city of Managua, Nicaragua. By evening, there were 6,000 dead, 20,000 injured, and 3,000 people without a place to stay. That night, Roberto met with a local TV producer named Luis Vigoreaux and a singer named Ruth Fernández. They talked about the disaster in Nicaragua, and they decided to form a committee to help the victims of the earthquake.

Through the Christmas season, Roberto worked day and night to raise money, medicine, clothing, and food for the people of Nicaragua. Only a few weeks earlier, he had visited Managua as the manager of a Puerto Rican amateur baseball team. He made many friends there, including a fourteen-year-old boy who had lost both legs in an accident. When Roberto discovered that the boy needed $750 for a pair of artificial legs, he and the players on his team put up the money.

By New Year's Eve, there had already been three flights to Managua with relief supplies. The people of Puerto Rico were doing all they could to help their Latin American neighbors. But then Roberto heard reports that the supplies were not all going to the people who needed them. He decided to fly with the next shipment to see what was happening for himself.

"If I go to Nicaragua," he said, "the stealing will stop. They would not dare to steal from Roberto Clemente."

New Year's Eve is a time of great joy in Puerto Rico. It is the most important holiday of the year— a time when families gather together and share the good food and drink of their table. Vera did not want Roberto to leave for Managua until after the new year. But Roberto felt he had to go.

"It is the least I can do," he said. "Babies are dying over there. They need these supplies." They decided he would leave that afternoon as he had planned. "Just be sure to have roast pork for me and the kids when I get back," he said.

Roberto and Vera went to the airport around 3:30 that afternoon. The cargo plane, loaded with food and medical supplies, was supposed to leave at 4:00. But it was an old plane, and they were having mechanical problems. At 5:00, Vera kissed Roberto good-bye and went to pick up some friends who were coming in from Pennsylvania. She assumed that Roberto's plane would be leaving soon.

Roberto Jr. and the other Clemente children were staying at Vera's mother's house in Carolina. As he was getting ready to go to bed, Roberto Jr., who was called Robertito, turned to his grandmother and said, "Grandma, Grandma, Papá is going to Nicaragua, and he won't be back. That plane is going to crash." Robertito was only seven years old. His grandmother calmed him down and tucked him into bed.

On the other side of Carolina, Don Melchor woke from an evening nap. He turned to Doña Luisa who was sitting nearby. "I had a dream that the airplane crashed into the sea," he said. Don Melchor was 91 years old. He was ill, and he needed his rest. "Go back to sleep," said Doña Luisa.

At 9:22 P.M., after a delay of over five hours, the old DC-7 cargo plane finally took off for Managua. There were five people on board, including Roberto. Within moments after take-off, there was a loud explosion and one of the four engines caught fire. The pilot tried to turn the plane around and head back to the airport, but it was too late. There were two more explosions and then another as the plane disappeared into the Atlantic a mile off the shore of Puerto Rico. Roberto Clemente was gone.

A Gift from Roberto

New Year's Day was cloudy and cool. A fine drizzle fell along the Atlantic Coast of Puerto Rico. Out in the choppy seas, boats and helicopters searched for signs of the wrecked plane. Along with the Navy divers, Manny Sanguillen dove again and again into the deep dark water, looking for Roberto's body. On the shore, Vera Clemente stood among thousands of people watching the rescue operations, hoping desperately for a miracle that never came.

The next day, Rafael Hernández Colón, the newly elected governor of Puerto Rico, cancelled his inauguration celebrations and declared three days of mourning. "Roberto died serving his fellow man," said Colón. "Our youth loses an idol and an example. Our people lose one of their glories."

On January 4, a memorial service was held in the same church where Roberto and Vera had been married. All of the Pittsburgh Pirates flew down to Puerto Rico for the service. Roberto's old managers Harry Walker and Danny Murtaugh were there, along with Baseball Commissioner Bowie Kuhn. "He had a touch of royalty about him," Kuhn said after the service. "He made the word 'superstar' seem inadequate. And what a wonderfully good man he was."

In Pittsburgh, there was another memorial service attended by 1,300 people. A neon sign that usually advertised beer was changed so its message would read: "Adios Amigo." (Good-bye, Friend.) In the emptiness of Three Rivers Stadium, the scoreboard simply said: "Roberto Clemente 1934–1972."

After eleven days of diving in the rough seas, the search was called off. The divers had found the wreckage of the plane and the body of the pilot. Roberto's briefcase washed ashore a week later. Roberto's body was never found.

At the Pirates' training camp in Bradenton, Florida, a plaque was placed on the door of Roberto's room. On the plaque were these words: "I want to be remembered as a ballplayer who gave all he had to give." It was signed "Roberto Clemente."

On March 20, 1973, less than three months after his death, Roberto Clemente was elected into the

Baseball Hall of Fame. Normally a player must wait five years after his career is over before he can be elected. But the Baseball Writers Association of America voted to make an exception for Roberto. On August 6, he was officially enshrined in the Hall of Fame at Cooperstown. Among the other men admitted to the Hall on that day was Monte Irvin, Roberto's boyhood idol.

On opening day of the 1973 season, Roberto's number 21 was officially retired in a special ceremony at Three Rivers Stadium. Ruth Fernández sang the Puerto Rican national anthem. "When you honor Roberto Clemente," she said, "you honor all of Puerto Rico." The Pirates came from behind to defeat the St. Louis Cardinals 7–5. Manny Sanguillen played right field.

Fifteen years later, through the hard work of Vera Clemente and the Puerto Rican people, the *Ciudad Deportiva* stands on 600 acres of land between Carolina and San Juan. Roberto's dream has become a reality. There are six baseball fields, two basketball courts, tennis courts, a swimming pool, a batting cage, dormitories, and a recreation area. More facilities are being built.

The Sports City is not yet finished, but it is already being used by the children of Puerto Rico.

It is free, and it is open to all. It doesn't matter who they are or how much money they have or what is the color of their skin. It is a place where young people can learn to be better human beings through the power of sports. It is a gift from Roberto.

BIBLIOGRAPHY

Angell, Roger, *The Summer Game*, The Viking Press, 1972.

Bims, Hamilton, "Roberto Clemente: Sad End for a Troubled Man," *Ebony*, March 1973.

Blount, Roy, Jr., "No Disgruntlements Round Here," *Sports Illustrated*, August 10, 1970; "On the Lam with the Three Rivers Gang," *Sports Illustrated*, August 2, 1971; "Roberto Clemente: Death of a Proud Man," *Sports Illustrated*, January 15, 1973; "Now Playing Right: Manny Sanguillen," *Sports Illustrated*, March 19, 1973.

Bonventre, Peter, "Roberto the Great," *Newsweek*, January 15, 1973.

Brosnan, Jim, *The Long Season*, Harper & Brothers, Publishers, 1960.

Cáceres, Maria Isabel, "Unforgettable Roberto Clemente," *Reader's Digest*, July 1973.

Clemente, Luis, telephone interview, June 13, 1987.

Clemente, Vera, telephone interviews, May 31, 1987 and June 11, 1987.

Cope, Myron, "Aches and Pains and Three Batting Titles," *Sports Illustrated*, March 7, 1966.

Current Biography, Vol. 33, No. 2 (February 1972), The H. W. Wilson Company, 1972.

Grossman, Edward, "Pride of the Pirates," *Commentary*, January 1974.

Hano, Arnold, *Roberto Clemente: Batting King*, G. P. Putnam's Sons, 1968.

Harman, Carter, *The West Indies*, "Experiment in Reform," Time Incorporated, 1966.

James, Bill, *The Bill James Historical Baseball Abstract*, Villard Books, 1986.

Kahn, Roger, *A Season in the Sun*, "The Children of Roberto," Harper & Row, Publishers, 1977.

Life, "The Bucs Heist Series and the Lid Blows Off," October 24, 1960.

Manley, Effa and Hardwick, Leon Herbert, *Negro Baseball . . . Before Integration*, Adams Press, 1976.

Masterson, Dave, *Baseball's Best: The MVPs*, Contemporary Books, 1985.

Miller, Ira, *Roberto Clemente*, Tempo Books, Grosset & Dunlap, 1973.

Musick, Phil, *Who Was Roberto?* Doubleday & Company, Inc., 1974.

Newsweek, "Champagne and Aspirin," October 25, 1971; "Champions of the World," October 24, 1960.

New York Times, various articles, 1955–1972.

Official Baseball Guide, 1986 edition, The Sporting News, 1986.

Official World Series Records, The Sporting News, 1982.

Pittsburgh Pirates, Roberto Clemente Night program, July 24, 1970.

Ritter, Lawrence and Honig, Donald, *The 100 Greatest Baseball Players of All Time*, Crown Publishers, 1981.

Rudeen, Kenneth, *Roberto Clemente*, Thomas Y. Crowell Company, 1974.

San Francisco Chronicle, various articles, July 1961 and October 1971.

Siwoff, Seymour, *The Book of Baseball Records*, Seymour Siwoff, 1980.

Slater, Mary, *The Caribbean Islands*, The Viking Press, 1968.

Time, "Whammy with a Weenie," August 12, 1966; "Old Aches & Pains," May 26, 1967; "Requiem for Roberto," January 15, 1973.

Turkin, Hy and Thompson, S. C. *The Official Encyclopedia of Baseball*, Doubleday & Company, Inc., 1977.

Wagenheim, Kal, *Clemente!* Praeger Publishers, 1973.

Ways, C. R., " 'Nobody Does Anything Better Than Me in Baseball' says Roberto Clemente . . . Well, He's Right," *The New York Times Magazine*, April 19, 1972.

Wolf, David, "The Strain of Being Roberto Clemente," *Life*, May 21, 1968.

Roberto Clemente's Career Record

Year	G	AB	R	H	2B	3B	HR	RBI	SO	BB	SB	BA	SA
1955	124	474	48	121	23	11	5	47	60	18	2	.255	.382
1956	147	543	66	169	30	7	7	60	58	13	6	.311	.431
1957	111	451	42	114	17	7	4	30	45	23	0	.253	.348
1958	140	519	69	150	24	10	6	50	41	31	8	.289	.408
1959	105	432	60	128	17	7	4	50	51	15	2	.296	.396
1960	144	570	89	179	22	6	16	94	72	39	4	.314	.458
1961	146	572	89	201	30	10	23	100	59	35	4	.351	.559
1962	144	538	95	168	28	9	10	74	73	35	6	.312	.454
1963	152	600	77	192	23	8	17	76	64	31	12	.320	.470
1964	155	622	95	211	40	7	12	87	87	51	5	.339	.484
1965	152	589	91	194	21	14	10	65	78	43	8	.329	.463
1966	154	638	105	202	31	11	29	119	109	46	7	.317	.536
1967	147	585	103	209	26	10	23	110	103	41	9	.357	.554
1968	132	502	74	146	18	12	18	57	77	51	2	.291	.482
1969	138	507	87	175	20	12	19	91	73	56	4	.345	.544
1970	108	412	65	145	22	10	14	60	66	38	3	.352	.556
1971	132	522	82	178	29	8	13	86	65	26	1	.341	.502
1972	102	378	68	118	19	7	10	60	49	29	0	.312	.479
18	2433	9454	1416	3000	440	166	240	1305	1230	621	83	.317	.475

Playoff Record

Year	G	AB	R	H	2B	3B	HR	RBI	SO	BB	SB	BA	SA
1970	3	14	1	3	0	0	0	1	4	0	0	.214	.214
1971	4	18	2	6	0	0	0	4	6	1	0	.333	.333
1972	5	17	1	4	1	0	1	2	5	3	0	.235	.471
3	12	49	4	13	1	0	1	7	15	4	0	.265	.347

World Series Record

Year	G	AB	R	H	2B	3B	HR	RBI	SO	BB	SB	BA	SA
1960	7	29	1	9	0	0	0	3	4	0	0	.310	.310
1971	7	29	3	12	2	1	2	4	2	2	0	.414	.759
2	14	58	4	21	2	1	2	7	6	2	0	.362	.534